WISE WORDS:

LESSONS IN ENTREPRENEURSHIP & VENTURE CAPITAL

VOLUME 1

BY SEAN EVAN WISE BA, LLB, MBA

ISBN: 978-1-4303-2930-5

First Published in 2007 by Lantern Productions.

Printed on demand by Lulu.com.

Design by Dixie Press.

This Book is Dedicated to:

My father, **Mel "Papa Joe" Wise** who taught me
that the true measure of man was determined not by how many times
he gets knocked down, but by how many times he gets back up
AND
To my mother, **Beverly Wise**, who taught me
"if it is to be, then it is up to me".

Inis,

Thanks for coming

Iris!

Thanks for coming

To err, is human.
To forgive, divine.
To pick yourself up after failure and try again,
Now that is an entrepreneur.

Sean Wise, 2007

Special Thanks:

This book would not have been possible without the contributions and support of so many. I'm sure that I will miss quite a few, notwithstanding, I would like to thank:

Paul Gilligan • Allison Hughes • Matt Henderson • John Goudey
Dennis Ensing • Dan Mothersill • Les Hansen • Stacey & Craig
Rudin • Madison & Jake Rudin • Suzanne Valles • Delilah Panino
Len Brody • Debbie Landa • Stuart Coxe • Joe Timlin • Deni Kosloff
Dixie Press • Al & Gert Wise and of course,
Mr. Clarke (my junior high school guidance counslor)

Table of Contents

Introduction By The Author

I would like to begin by thanking you for picking up this book. Assisting and informing entrepreneurs is truly a labour of love for me and I hope that you are able to share in my passion while digesting this collection.

I am the son of two very tenacious and succssful entrepreneurs and so, from an early age I knew that entrepreneurship was the path for me to pursue. I started my first business at the age of 16, entertaining children as a clown for kids' parties. Laugh as you may, but where else can a teenager make $50/hour with a two hour minimum? Since then, I have had 5 ventures, some of which were successsful, while others were less so.

From a professional standpoint, even as a young lawyer in Toronto, I knew it was the underdog entrepreneurs that I wanted to represent. This carried on as I moved from law to corporate finance and from corporate finance to venture capital.

My passion was only magnified when I began to lecture on the topics that I loved so much. It was at one such lecture that my long time editor at the Globe and Mail, Sasha Nagy, approached me and offered me to the opportunity to take my teachings to the world....well, at least to Canada.

Years later, I am hoping that he still thinks it was a good idea, but from the volume of comments and e-mails we both receive, I think we can reasonably conclude that it was.

What you are holding in your hands is the first (but hopefully not the last) volume of my columns. In this tome, I cover a variety of interesting topics and hopefully do so from a perspective that will appeal to you.

With the above in mind, I hope that you enjoy this book as much as I enjoyed writing each and every column. I welcome comments from each and every reader, you can reach me direct at WiseWords@WiseMentorCapital.com

Be Well,

Sean Wise, BA, MBA, LLB

Chapter 1

It Is Still Who You Know!

Originally Published September 19, 2005

Closing Venture Capital is a lot like consummating a marriage. It takes time for the relationship to mature and blossom. In today's connected economy, there are many ways to begin the courting process, but if you want to ensure your time is efficiently leveraged during the dating process it still comes down to "who you know."

I recently discussed this with a cross section of the Venture Capital (VC) professionals to determine where they got their deal flow and which source of deal flow had the highest probability of closing an investment. I spoke with Kirk Washington from Yaletown Ventures (a seed fund in Vancouver); Robin Axon from Ventures West (one of the country's oldest and most successful

> **Wise Words# 1**
> *Closing Venture Capital is a lot like consummating a marriage, it takes time for the relationship to mature and blossom.*

early stage funds) and Doug Hewson from Axis Capital (an Ottawa based seed fund), this is how they ranked their deal flow.

Unsolicited Submission

Probability of getting a meeting - 100:1;
Probability that a deal gets done - 1000:1

The fact is, you probably wouldn't go on a date with someone who called out of the blue and said "Hi, you don't know me, but I read about you on the internet and I really want to marry you, so can we have a date?" Well, that's how VCs view unsolicited business plans. Robin Axon of Ventures West offers this blunt assessment. *"We received more than 500 unsolicited business plans last year but met with very few. As for closing a deal, I don't think we've ever invested in a first-time entrepreneur's company that came in unsolicited."* The truth is, for most funds the little "submit plan here" button on their website is simply a way of screening out those who don't understand their business. After all, it is easier to delete electronic documents than those submitted by snail-mail.

Unknown Agent

Probability of getting a meeting - 50:1;
Probability that a deal gets done - 100:1

There are many posers out there claiming they can help you get business funding if only you agree to pay them $10,000 a month and 10 per cent of the money raised. However, that is exactly what they are, POSERS. In many cases, they have neither the relationships nor the license to deliver. In some cases, the only connection these so-called "agents" have with the VCs is that they met them at a cocktail party three years prior and kept their business card. These unlicensed agents know (and care) little about the Fund's mandate, financing criteria or investment approach. Often, they over-shop your business to anyone and everyone, effectively killing your chance of landing money as well as taxing your scarce time and resources. Furthering the courtship analogy, setups by unlicensed agents have about as much chance of leading to a long-term union, as a blind date set up by your great-great-grandmother.

Before you agree to work with anyone who offers to set you up with VCs be sure to ask four key questions:

- Are you a licensed Limited Market Dealer (the Securities Commissions want legitimate brokers to qualify and register if they are going to take contingency fees)?
- Which VCs can vouch for you?
- Which ones have you worked with?
- Which ventures did you fail to raise capital for?

(After all everyone loves their agent when they succeed, the better test is look at those CEOs who failed to raise capital and see how much weight they put on the Agents for the failure).

Venture Fairs, Financing Forums, And Other Industry Events

Probability of getting a meeting - 15:1;
Probability that a deal gets done - 20:1 -- much higher if you win "best in show"

Across Canada, there are a variety of trade associations striving to serve the emerging growth markets (the Toronto Venture Group, OCRI, CTI, etc.) most, if not all, have annual "dog and pony" beauty contests. Founders looking for money have 15 minutes to impress a room full of investors. Choosing which event to present is often a tough decision. The ultimate success you may find comes down to who is choosing the presenters.

If VCs select the presenters, then your chances of finding a match increase dramatically. However, if the companies are chosen by sponsors, industry professionals, or event organizers, your chances decline greatly. The reason why nearly 40 per cent of the presenting companies at the annual Canadian Venture Forum in Toronto go on to raise funds isn't the food CVF serves. The fact is that CVF presenters are handpicked by a selection committee of 30+ Tier One VCs based on their "fundability." Their "fundability" and the peer driven selection process in turn attracts more VCs to attend. This stacks the audience, which in turn, increases the probability of funding and the cycle perpetuates.

Professionals With Fund Relationships

Probability of getting a meeting - 3:1;
Probability that a deal gets done - 5:1

Venture Capital is all about relationships, particularly when it comes to deal flow. Those professional service providers with deep and meaningful relationships with the Funds are most acutely aware of the inner workings of the Funds you want to meet.

"The majority of our deal flow comes from our network of contacts," said Kirk Washington, of Yaletown Ventures.

These people understand exactly what particular VCs are looking for based on: stage of business, industry and geography and risk to return ratio, and this knowledge when combined with their long term relationship, allows them to more easily acquire the ear of the investor on your behalf. Further, the VCs know that these professionals work with them day in and day out and therefore are much less likely to agree to introduce companies that will damage the relationship. The VCs are, in turn, a large source of work for these professional service providers. Truth be told, no tier one service provider is going to trade their long-term relationships just to satisfy your short-term engagement.

I break these matchmakers up into three classes:

- accountants, who carry out audit and valuation work for the Funds themselves;

- lawyers, who undertake transaction support for the Funds;

- and limited market dealers, who get paid for closing deals.

There are two distinct differences between these professionals and the Posers described above: (1) each is a licensed professional, who must subscribe to an orderly code of conduct; and (2) each has a long term relationship to maintain with the Fund, a relationship they won't maintain if they bring consistently low quality deals to the VCs.

Current And Future Investors

Probability of getting a meeting - 2:1;
Probability that a deal gets done - 3:1

"I like it so much; our Fund is leading the round. You just have to meet them." These words, spoken by a Tier One VC, will usually get you a meeting with any VC, anywhere, any time. After all, the fact that one Fund is willing to write a cheque is often impetus enough for another VC to have a look-see. Most VCs will almost always take calls from their peers on deal flow.

However, it is also important to note that this call has to come directly from one VC to another. Too often I have heard, "well so-and-so VC is interested, so you should be too." Trust me. That isn't the same thing as, "I'm syndicating this deal, do you want to have a look?"

A call from a current investor is even better than a call from a future investor. Successful tech entrepreneurs are still a rare breed in Canada. However, rarely are winnings reinvested as in the form of Angel investment. For this reason, most VCs will take meetings from Angels on companies that they have sunk money into. After all, if it is good enough for the guy who founded Research in Motion, it is probably good enough for most VCs.

Stakeholder To The Fund

Probability of getting a meeting - 1:1;
Probability that a deal gets done - 3:1

There are two referral sources that beat out all the rest: investors in the Funds themselves and portfolio CEOs.

Funds, like entrepreneurs, have to raise money (and yes, karma does go around). In the case of private funds like JL Albright

> **Wise Words # 2**
> The easiest way to get a VC meeting is getting a warm referral from a CEO currently in the VC's portfolio.

and Ventures West, this money may come from institutions like Teachers' Private Capital and OMERS or Fund of Funds like the Business Development Bank of Canada which committed millions in capital and became an LP (Limited Partner) to the Fund. So you can bet when an LP, who has 10 per cent of a VC's $100-million fund, calls and asks him to take a meeting, he'll be there.

As Yaletown Venture's Kirk Washington said: *"Every cheque we wrote was to a lead that either came from an LP, another VC, or through our personal network."*

How does this help you? Unfortunately, it doesn't, since getting to the LPs is often more difficult than getting to the VCs. There is however an easier way.

The Bottom Line

The easiest way to get a VC meeting, and yet the most underutilized method, is getting a warm referral from a CEO of a VC backed portfolio company. After all, who better to endorse you than someone the VC trusts enough to invest $5-10 million into? Who knows better what that investor is looking for, than someone who has it? Further, these CEOs are readily accessible (they can be found just by clicking through the portfolios section on the VC's website) Best of all, entrepreneurs love to talk about their business, especially their successes. So if you want to meet a VC, call up some of their current investors and ask them about their fundraising experiences. Worst case scenario you will find out more than you hoped about their investors; best case scenario they might offer to make the introduction.

After all, it still is who you know!

Chapter 2

Use A Rifle, Not A Shotgun, When Hunting Venture Capital

Originally Published October 12, 2005

It takes an exorbitant amount of time, money and mental bandwidth to raise capital. Under today's market conditions, one should expect to spend no less than six to nine months, $100,000 and 500 hours of senior management's time to prepare, target, pitch, negotiate, paper and close a venture capital financing (i.e. an investment of anywhere from $2-15 million from an institutional professional investor into an emerging growth company).

That is just the simple reality of attracting outside investors and then converting their interest in your opportunity into money in your company's bank account.

> **Wise Words # 3**
> *One of the biggest mistakes that entrepreneurs make in pursuing capital is over shopping or shotgunning their deal.*

Can you shorten the time frame? Yes, but only if you act counter-intuitively to your first instinct, and use a sniper's rifle and not a shotgun when targeting investors.

One of the biggest mistakes that entrepreneurs make in pursuing capital is over shopping or shot-gunning their deal. Most entrepreneurs, once they've put the finishing touches on their financial model, business plan, executive summary, elevator pitch and 12 slide investor presentation, feel the need to flog it to each and every person they meet.

These well intentioned entrepreneurs are hoping to rely on the old adage, 'if you throw enough stuff on the wall, something will probably stick." But, in reality, the best advisors know there are a limited number of sources of capital for each deal. Showing the deal to investors that have neither the interest nor the ability to do the deal is not only a waste of energy, it can also significantly lower the probability that any deal will get done. After all, Telus Ventures has little ability (or interest) in investing in a biotech deal, unless it is to put a phone inside someone's head, so why show that deal to them?

The dangers from shot-gunning your deals are multifold:

- Targeting too many investors often spreads the team too thin and forces you to cut coners in preparing for those investors who have a higher probability of doing the deal.

- Investors often wonder if the methodology for raising capital is indicative of how management will carry on business, particularly sales and strategic alliances.

- Management must balance its energy between running the company and pitching the company. Following low probability leads will not only become a distraction, but this will take the CEOs focus away from running the business.

- A company that pitches itself before entering an investor's sweet spot risks making a bad first impression. Unfortunately, although an investor may hear a company's pitch over 6, 12, and 18 months, and many things may improve, it is generally the first impression that they retain.

- The VC industry is incredibly small. Once a deal makes "the rounds," its reputation may actually begin to precede it and the company may be judged not on their true opportunity but on the perception they leave behind with the investor who in turn passes these views around like a cold. Investors may wonder just how good a deal can be if you have to sell it to so many firms.

So how do you increase the probability of getting a deal done without increasing the number of investors you pitch to? Focus on quality not quantity!

There are several key steps that can both increase the probability of your venture raising funds and dramatically decrease the cost of doing so.

Step 1: Prepare

Before you can even start the process of raising money you have to understand not only your business backwards and forwards, but you have to understand the key metrics of the opportunity you are showing - so ask yourself the following:

- How much capital does this venture need to succeed? Is that sum needed all at once or can it be tied to milestones?

- What milestones are ahead over the next 6, 12, and 18 months (first sales, break even, market adoption)?

- What are the "use of funds" (finish R&D, rollout product, expand sales force)?

- Is this a seed (pre sales), early stage (sales of $0.5- 2M), or later stage (sales of $2M+) venture?

Once you know the answers to these questions you know what sort of deal you are taking to market.

Step 2: Target

Different sources of capital like different sorts of deals. According to Jeff Park from Covington Capital, you need to know your audience. *"Who is in the room, which deals have they, or their firm done. Each investor looks at prospective investments from slightly different aspects: some examine intellectual property and patents, others focus on channel partners or historical customers, while others mostly care about some newly signed contracts,"* said Mr. Park.

In order to determine what each VC is looking for, you need to do more than just read their website and press releases. Almost all VCs in this country call themselves "early stage capital," but each has distinctly different definitions of the term. In order to really see an investor's focus, review their investments over the last 12-18 months to determine the characteristics those investments share.

But past history doesn't always determine future activity. One should also simultaneously delve deep into the current state of the fund they wish to pitch to. In doing so, determine:

- The type of fund it is (Government, Limited Partner, Labour sponsored, corporate, bank owned, debt, etc.).

- What is their investment mandate (by stage, industry, geography, etc.).

- Where in the lifecycle the fund is at often dictates the investment activity level of the fund (i.e. LP funds in the seventh year may not be looking for new deals, Labour sponsored funds typically fundraise annually in Ql and thus aren't focused on new deals).

- What level of traction the fund typically requires its investments to have hit before it is willing to consider making an investment (patents, customers, revenues, etc.).

- How much dry powder (i.e. cash on hand) the fund has left, and determine if this capital is already tentatively committed to current portfolio companies.

- The bandwidth currently available internally (most seed funds can take on 1-3 investments per investment manager, most early stage funds 3-5 per, some late stage funds 5-7 per).

You can find out most of this information on-line from www.CanadaVC.com or from www.NVCA.org or by speaking with the fund themselves or with those that have close relationships in the industry.

Once you know the lay of the land, you should try and match up only with investors directly interested in companies with your characteristics. You need to rifle in on only those sources of capital that can do, and are doing, deals like yours. I think Sunil Selby from Trellis Capital says it best: *"Since the VC process is time consuming, an entrepreneur is more likely to 'hit the bull's eye' by concentrating their efforts on those VC's whose criteria they fit. Knowing these criteria expedites the process and reflects well on the entrepreneur, confidence in whom is a significant factor in the investment decision process."*

Step 3: Recruit An Introduction

As discussed in a previous WISE WORDS column, venture capital is a business of relationships. If you want your deal to be reviewed you need an introduction from a source the VC trusts. Deals that come from trusted sources have a much higher probability of not only getting reviewed but of getting done. Deals that come in cold, generally do not. Remember the words of Ventures West Vice-President Robin Axon. *"We received more than 500 unsolicited business plans last year ... I don't think we've ever invested in a ... company that came in unsolicited."*

What is the best way to get this key introduction? Review the VCs current portfolio and go and meet with CEOs that your target investor has already funded. These executives, not so long ago, were in your exact situation. Worst case scenario - you learn more about the VC; best case scenario - they agree to introduce you.

Step 4: Customize

Many entrepreneurs simply rehash the same slide deck over and over. Although this approach is way too often the norm, Mr. Park strongly believes this is the wrong way to go.

"Entrepreneurs need to remind themselves when was the last time they had millions of dollars on the line from a presentation. For most of them it would be never!" said Mr. Park. *"By researching who you are presenting to, and truly understanding them, you can better position yourself for success."*

Our firm recommends that you apply some of the research you have learned and customize each presentation to each investor. We always mentor our clients to insert two slides at the very beginning of each presentation. The first, showing why you are pitching that particular investor and outlining how what you are looking for fits with what they are looking for (timing, amount, ROI), thereby potentially aligning interests amongst investor and investee. The second slide focuses on the investor's existing portfolio, showing how an investment in your venture not only resembles an investment in their current portfolio companies (by stage, industry, customer base) but also showing how, by making an investment in you, you may potentially enhance the ROI on the investments in them (through strategic alliances, potential M&A, and shared mindset). Adding these slides shows investors that you aren't shot gunning your deal willy-nilly but instead applying resources judiciously (just as you will with their money), and shows that you are not only aware of what their fund is up to, but are interested in being part of their portfolio. Finally, it also shows that you know how *to do business.*

The Bottom Line

Following these steps won't necessarily get you funding, but it will make the pursuit of capital much more efficient. Financing is a quality not a quantity game. After all, when hunting elusive prey, you need to use a sniper's rifle, not a shotgun.

Chapter 3

Networking As A Factor Of Commercial Evolution

Originally published November 17, 2005

Over 150 years ago, Charles Darwin proposed that evolution only allows those with the traits necessary to survive to flourish. For example: In nature's ecosystem only those burgeoning entities that possess the ability to forage for food and protect against hostile environmental factors can survive. This is the same for the modern commercial ecosystem with regard to start-ups. Only those start-ups with the skills to find the necessary elements of life will flourish. Just as a baby bear must forage for food or die of starvation, a startup company must likewise forage for key resources (capital, human talent and client traction) while still in its infancy. Failure to obtain these necessary elements of business is seen by the capital markets as a sign that the entity does not have what it takes to grow into a dominant force in its ecosystem.

> **Wise Words # 4**
> *An entrepreneur's ability to network can determine whether the venture succeeds or starves to death.*

But how does a startup company with little or no capital gather the resources it needs to grow? The answer: **Networking.**

17

In the business world, an entrepreneur's ability to network can often determine whether the venture succeeds or starves to death. Often times, entrepreneurs do not realize the power that a strong professional network offers. Never are these skills more needed than when you simply cannot afford the necessary elements of life. During this "bootstrapping" phase, you have no choice but to forage (or network) for them.

But how does one network effectively? What are the rules to networking? How can you get what you need when you simply cannot afford it? When it comes to networking there are many rules, but here are the four that I have found most effective:

Rule #1: Take Every Meeting

John Goudey, a Senior Partner at Ernst & Young and widely considered one of the most connected people in the Toronto business scene, mentored me for several years. During that time he imparted many pearls of wisdom, but the most sage piece of advice was simply, *"Take Every Meeting."*

If anyone wants to meet and discuss strategic alliances, working together, or simply share where their business is at, it is important to take the meeting. Goudey said there were three reasons to do this, even if you cannot immediately see the benefit or figure out, "what is in it for me?"

(a) Even if the person you are meeting with cannot add value to what you are doing, you simply never know who in their network might. There are, after all, only six degrees of separation in the modern world.

(b) You always meet the same people on the way up as you do on the way down, so be courteous to everyone. One day, even if it is not today, they might be of useful contact.

(c) It is simply the right thing to do. Enlightened self interest can be a powerful motivator, but selflessly serving others, even if it never results in a direct benefit to you or your enterprise, is still worth undertaking in its own right. Think of a time in your career where you wished someone was there to open a door for you or to give you a leg up. Why not use this opportunity to be that person for someone else?

In my practice, I take more than a dozen meetings a month with people who want something from me or my firm. Seldom do these meetings result in immediate results, but by taking them, I have the opportunity to learn about what others are up to and consequently set the scene for future gain. At a minimum, I get the opportunity to do the right thing and help others. At a maximum, I might find something that can one day be of use to me. After all, if you are willing to help others succeed, you will most likely develop a fan club that will evangelise your good name and, in the future, will genuinely want to help you succeed in return.

> **Wise Words # 5**
> *For any commercial relationship to be sustainable their must be balance. For balance, there must be an alignment of interests.*

Rule #2: Find Alignment

Networking is not a one way street. Always asking for what you need, instead of determining how both parties can benefit, is the surest way to stifle your network potential. For any commercial relationship to be sustainable, there must be balance. To achieve balance there must first be an alignment of interests.

Dale Carnegie's *"How to Win Friends and Influence People,"* reminds us that most people only see their own perspective. They can only ask WIFM(What Is in it For Me). Carnegie reminds us that if we want others to act for our benefit, we have to be able to formulate our request in terms of how it actually helps the other person. For example, if you are applying for a job, do not sell your future employer on why you need the job, but instead show your next boss how acquiring your talents will help him or her to meet the company's goals.

So when you meet with others, either formally or informally, strive to learn about their business, its goals, its needs and its model. And while doing so, take a genuine interest in their backgrounds and what they have to tell you. Rushing through the conversation just to get what you are looking for leaves a poor impression. Try to put yourself in their shoes and turn your mind to what you can do to advance their opportunity. Try to find out what their key metrics are and give some thought to how those intertwine with what you are trying to accomplish.

> **Wise Words # 6**
> *By providing utility to someone, you have a better chance of getting fed yourself.*

Casey Shea, President of Earthworx, and in my estimation, one of the finest net workers I have ever met, put it this way: "My strategy has always been to know who is who and what THEY need to survive. By providing utility to someone, you have a better chance of getting fed yourself."

Once you have been able to gain this understanding, try to facilitate the reverse. Help them to understand what you and your firm are trying to accomplish and what you might currently lack to get there. This is a great opportunity to use what Leonard Brody, author of one of this year's entrepreneurial must reads, *"Everything I Needed to Know About Business ... I Learned from a Canadian"* calls the Entrepreneurial Jedi Mind Trick: *"Most seasoned entrepreneurs utilize a charisma that allows them to rally people around their cause; a sort of gravitational pull that makes people want to help and get involved. A feeling like if they don't, they are missing out on something truly meaningful".*

Rule #3: Go First

If you have ever been pitched on a strategic alliance, then you know that these meetings usually end with both sides pledging a commitment to help the other. Well-meaning intentions aside, too often this never happens. Too many people adopt a "wait and see" approach. They say to themselves "Well, let's see how much value they bring to us before we spend any energy helping bring value to them." This is, in my estimation, the wrong way to proceed.

Instead, GO FIRST! Develop goodwill by acting on this new potential "alliance" by sending over a sales lead, sharing some pertinent information or inviting them to meet someone from your network that could assist them. By going first you are adding to the ""goodwill bank account"," an account that you might later be able to draw down upon. In this way, networking is more akin to farming than hunting, or as Matt Henderson, Director of Business Development for Ernst & Young's Pacific region, puts it: "Networking is like gardening. You plant the seed by providing something of value to someone you wish to build a relation-

21

ship with, while asking nothing in return. You then continue to nurture the relationship by giving ongoing care and attention: a thoughtful note, a valuable contact, an invitation to an event, sharing some key insight. Then as the relationship begins to flower and grow due to the time and attention you have paid to it, it begins to bear valuable fruit. Fruit that when the time is right, you can pick and use to nourish your pursuits".

Rule #4: Pick The Fruit Only When It Is Ripe

One of the greatest networking mistakes you can make is cashing out your goodwill account incorrectly. You can bankrupt your goodwill account by: asking for something unreasonable, asking for something too soon or simply asking for too much.

You should never ask for a favour from someone in your network when it is either not in their best interest to give, beyond their efficacy, or goes against their model, metrics and goals. For example, you should never ask an auditor to give your firm a free audit. After all, audits are primarily what they get paid for. Instead, you could ask your accountant for a copy of that firm's most recent research report, an introduction to a source of capital they do work for or an invitation to an event they are hosting.

> **Wise Words # 7**
> *You should never ask for a favor that is not in their best interest to give, beyond their efficacy, or goes against their goals.*

All those items are secondary to the primary goal of their firm – sell more audit services - and so asking for something like a free audit is not only impossible but it shows that you really did not understand rule #2.

Cashing in favours too soon or worse yet, too often, both can be monstrously detrimental to your network. After all, if you pick a tree too bare, there won't be any fruit seeds left to replenish what was taken, or as Matt Henderson says, "Networking is like gardening ... if you want to eat off of the relationship vine, you need to nurture it for the long haul".

The Bottom Line

More than a century and a half ago, Darwin wrote that those without the necessary traits for survival would naturally be weaned out of the ecosystem, and the same can be said today with regard to under-funded, early stage growth companies. Those that cannot bootstrap and acquire the elements of life through networking surely won't survive.

Chapter 4

The Double Dip: How To Build Once, Sell Twice And Make Money Three Times

Originally published December 13, 2005

How would you like to build something once, but get paid twice? How about getting paid three times for undertaking the same action? It is possible – if you know how to "double dip."

In the mid-80s, my father, Mel "Papa Joe" Wise – a long time car-guy and serial entrepreneur in his own right, learned that the population of a small South American country had a real need for used tires. Apparently, while they had many automobiles, nearly each and every one was older than he was. Consequently, the people needed a wide variety of auto parts (including tires), to keep these vehicles in service and on the road. Serendipitously, one of the provinces at the time was having a real problem storing excessive used tires in its landfills. So the idea struck my father: if he could acquire the tires from the province for little or nothing, then ship these tires to South America and sell them, he could make a tidy profit. However his potential profit skyrocketed when he discovered that the used tire problem was so significant, that this government would actually pay him to take as many tires as he could off their hands. Let me repeat for clarity: Someone was going to pay him to remove an item – the exact same item – that someone else was going to pay him to acquire. This concept of "build once, sell twice," was my fathers first encounter with what he would later term "the double dip."

Double dipping, at its core, refers to the ability to generate multiple revenue streams from the same expenditure of resources. Recognize however, that this model isn't limited to tires; nor is it limited to double dipping. In fact, if you are really strategic, you can often structure your business model to yield double, triple, and even quadruple dips. Look at the following to see how my dad could have made even more money off of the tire transaction:

> **Wise Words # 8**
> *Double Dipping refers to the ability to generate multiple revenue stems from the same expenditure of resources.*

1 Tire, 2 Transactions, 4 Ways To Make Money

The Single Dip: Sell used tires to a buyer looking for used tires.

The Double Dip: Be paid to remove used tires from landfills and other storage sites. Then sell those same used tires to buyer.

The Triple Dip: Receive a federal grant to set up a "green" environmental services company focused on helping to deal with the "used tire" problem. Be paid to remove used tires from landfill and other storage sites. Then sell those same used tires to a buyer.

The Quadruple Dip: Receive grant to set up a "green" environmental services company focused on helping deal with the "used tire" problem. Be paid to remove used tires from landfill and other storage sites. Then sell those same tires to a buyer looking for used tires. Do all of the above at a facility paid for through matching provincial grants to encourage economic development in an underutilized urban region.

Here are some more common examples:

- If you are selling new mattresses to the public and want to encourage sales, offer a trade-in program, whereby anyone bringing in their old mattress gets 15 percent off the price of a new mattress. Then turn around and donate the mattress to shelters and other excellent community organizations and claim the tax benefit for the donation. Then use your "charitable" act to raise the community profile of your mattress store, yielding free promotional coverage.

- If you are an IT consultancy, develop a product for a specific client, but retain the right to resell the tech you develop. Then, once deployed, sell the solution to other clients. Then, further dip by using government programs such as IRAP and SRED to help offset the development costs of the original project.

- If you are making a $100-million plus sci-fi blockbuster, make sure you leverage your production costs by monetizing all the ancillary markets. George Lucas, a veteran double dipper, may in the end have made more money from merchandising (action figures, books, t-shirts, video games, etc.) than from the box office.

If you want a more recent example, you need look no further than … Google. Google has made a killing from double dipping. After all, at its core, Google really only has two key assets: a proprietary search engine technology and tens of millions of people using that engine. But in the last year, Google has used both to leverage and expand their business model with the launch of Google desktop, Google maps, local search, froogle, keyhole, gmail and so much more, showing that the company is not simply going to rely on its click through/eyeball/ad words revenue model, but instead is going to leverage its millions of hits a day to massively double dip.

So how can you maximize your business model to generate the highest revenues possible through double dipping? The key is continually turning your deal on its ear until you can see all the possible variations and permutations. Asking a few key questions can help ensure that you don't leave anything on the table. I recommend that you always ponder these three questions to ask before signing a deal:

1. Have I fully monetized the primary revenue stream to allow for sustainability? i.e. Is there enough money in the deal to sustain the company should no other sources of revenue evolve?
2. From an external perspective, who else benefits from my primary transaction? i.e. Who else would pay to see us do what we plan to do anyway? From an internal perspective, what secondary benefits does my transaction throw off, and can I monetize such? i.e. Are there bi-products that result from the task? To whom can I sell such?
3. What small tweaks can I make to my business model to access and generate different forms of revenue? How can I increase revenue by making only minimum changes?

We most often see the double dip with technology and life science companies who out-license. Jeff Courtney, Partner at one of the country's leading investment funds, VenGrowth Private Equity Partners recognizes the value of out licensing.

THE DOUBLE DIP: HOW TO BUILD ONCE, SELL TWICE AND MAKE MONEY THREE TIMES

"Two things that start-up ventures are almost always seeking are cash, and validation of their technology or product. One effective strategy for achieving both is to out license part of the company's product portfolio," Said Courtney.

"If the company has more than one product, this often takes the form of out licensing one of its non-core products. Where the product portfolio is limited, the effective strategy may be to license the same product more than once. In its simplest form, this may be a license for rights to the product in a limited geographic territory such as Asia, or Europe. In perhaps a more complicated form, this might mean licensing the same product for different indications or target markets. In the case of a drug discovery, this could be the license for a topical form of the drug, keeping the oral form for the company," he said.

"Out licensing generates new revenue from additional applications of already expended resources, it allows high growth companies to build once and sell twice, and does so while also providing validation for the tech. Out licensing is a key strategy for maximized ROI."

However, double dipping is actually more than just maximizing returns. Double dipping is also about minimizing risk. In venture capital, where I do most of my work, most investors seek business models that have the potential to generate "multiple shots on the net." That is to say, venture capitalists are loathe to invest in companies that have "all their eggs in one basket." They know that a slight shift in any market ecosystem can leave their investee without a revenue stream, and might devastate any ROI they were initially seeking. Tim Lee, Vice-President of Investments from Growthworks, puts it this way: *"Active exploration of double dipping is vital for start-ups. The primary benefit is that it generates incremental revenues that leverage already limited resources. But the exercise also helps prevent tunnel vision, thereby allowing management to consistently revisit business and models. Most investors know more than their fair share of successful exits where the source of revenues at the end had little resemblance to the original business plan."*

The Bottom Line

Would you like to have a back-up plan in case the primary markets that you sell to suddenly change? Would you like to build something once, but make money from it twice? Three times? Would you like to maximize revenues and mitigate risk at the same time? If you have said yes to any of these questions, then you want to learn what "Papa Joe" Wise learned all those years ago, you want to learn how to double dip!

Chapter 5

Think You Can Talk Like A VC?
Don't Be Such A Blowfish

Originally published January 11, 2006

Entrepreneurs often complain that the rules of financing are seldom explained, let alone readily apparent. At the same time, most entrepreneurs do not have a financing thesaurus let alone a copy of the rulebook. Like most professions, Venture Capitalists (VCs) speak in their own language, one that is full of nuances and colloquialisms that many company founders never fully understand.

Wise Words is proud to present our picks for the top insider terms for Venture Capital in 05:

ROI: (Return on Investment). The term describes how much money the VCs make from a specific investment. (Ex. Investing $5M and receiving $50M on exit is a 9x ROI.)

Portfolio Company: (investee). A company that a VC has invested in. These companies often get classified as *stars, dogs and zombies* based on their ROI.

Star: A *portfolio company* that generates 5-10x RO1 upon exit.

Walking Dead/Zombie: A *portfolio company* that can only generate an *ROI*, equal to the amount of money invested into it.

Dog: A portfolio company that has no chance of returning any money to its investors. **Kennel Capital**: A portfolio of *dogs*.

Dogcatcher: A VC whose portfolio is kennel capital.

Eat your own Dogfood: When a company uses its own products for day-to-day operations. **Note:** doing so does not make you a *dog*, unless of course you are the only ones *eating your dog food*.

Angel: An individual, usually a serial entrepreneur, who invests regularly in extremely early-stage companies, before the VCs.

ArchAngel: A serial Angel investor, who has, to date, invested in a number of *stars*.

Been to the Dance: An entrepreneur who has succeeded in growing his company and generating a high *ROI* exit.

Blamestorming: Entrepreneurs and VCs fighting over who is at fault as a *portfolio company* shifts and begins to fall apart.

Blowfish: An early-stage (often pre-revenue) start-up entrepreneur who claims that his company makes better chips than Intel, better software than Microsoft and who knows more about customers and their needs than Dell.

Conservative Estimate: Overly optimistic financial forecasts that inexperienced first-time entrepreneurs generate using Excel.

Exit: A liquidity event (usually IPO or Sale) at which time the VCs are able to get their money out and generate an *ROI*.

Hockey Stick: Refers to 5- year pro-formas showing a year-over-year increase that when graphed as revenue vs. time looks like a hockey stick. Note: American VCs call this a moonshot.

OPM: Other People's Money.

Smoking OPM: Management's tendency to over-spend when they do not write a cheque alongside the VCs.

Runway: The number of months (or in some cases weeks) that a company has left, based on current actual cash on hand, before they run out of money and have to close down.

Flaming Out: When a company's *runway* ends abruptly. This is often the result of overspending in a grandiose way or the result of management smoking *OPM*.

Death by a Thousand Paper Cuts: When a company runs out of *runway* over a long period of time due to multiple small failures. The opposite of *flaming out*. The term can also be used to describe management's disdain for having to meet the extraordinary and tedious reporting requirements of some particular VCs.

Pipeline: A funnel diagram outlining possible upcoming sales over the near- and mid-term. It usually has a probability analysis built in to allow the reader to comfortably calculate the probable sales over the upcoming quarter.

Putting Lipstick on the Pig: When an entrepreneur tries to create a positive spin on a negative event, (ex. Our management team leaving at this time affords us an opportunity to retool our entire business focus and go-to-market plans). It can also be used to describe a bad product that is re- launched with new dressed- up front-end or the process in which a VC will over spin a *portfolio company's* story to facilitate a high exit.

Noisy Sales: Individual sales of a customized solution to a diverse customer set who will not pay more for the extra work, thus eroding margins. VCs will not pay huge multiples for these types of sales because they are not *scalable.*

Scalable: The ability to sell the 100th widget, at a much higher margin than the 1st widget. VCs love scalability because, as more and more units come off the line, costs do not ramp up as fast as revenue. On-line shareware is one of the most *scalable* product lines; while professional services is one of the least.

Shopped: (overshopped). A venture that has unsuccessfully attempted to raise capital, often over a long period, and thus was presented to more VCs than necessary.

Sweat Equity: The amount of time, energy and opportunity cost invested into a venture by the founders, for which no compensation (other than equity), was ever allocated and which most VCs discount entirely.

That is so 90s: A venture pitched as if the dot-com bubble never burst. These pitches often feature the *hockey stick, conservative estimates* and phrases such as "we have no competition" and "if we only get 2 per cent of the market".

Thin Green Line: The imaginary line that separates entrepreneurs from those in the VC industry. Those behind the line tend to stick together and are aghast when anyone breaks the code by revealing the truth behind the scenes.

Valuation: The agreed monetary figure on which the investment is made (i.e. if a VC invests $2 million and gets 30 per cent of the company, the *pre money valuation.* before investing was $4 million and the *post money valuation* is $6 million). Valuations are always too low from the founders' perspective, and often too high from the investors.

Vulture Capital: VCs with reputations of taking advantage of entrepreneurs, by either taking too much equity, giving one sided term sheets or unreasonably low *valuation.*

The Bottom Line

So there you have it. Your first exposure to the wacky world of VC speak. Need other terms or phrases defined? Want to know the difference between: a milestone and a tranche? A cramdown and a ratchet? An RTO and an IPO? Have other financing questions you want answered?

Feel free to write me at WiseWords@WisementorCapital.com

Chapter 6

Clamo, Ergo Sum

(I Pitch, Therefore I Am)

Originally published February 10, 2006

Guy Kawasaki tells us in his bestselling entrepreneurial guide The Art of the Start (one of my "Entrepreneurial Top 5 Must Reads for 2005"), that Rene Descartes' principle "I think, therefore I am," in the case of Entrepreneurs, should really be "I pitch, therefore I am." He goes on to tell the old investor joke "How do you know when an entrepreneur is pitching? His lips are moving."

For entrepreneurs, a good pitch is needed no matter the task at hand. Want to raise capital? –You need to pitch your plan. Want to attract top notch employees? – you need to pitch your vision. Want to attract strategic partners? – You need to pitch the benefits of working with you. Want to increase sales? – You need to pitch your solution.

> **Wise Words # 9**
> *The ability to pitch in a meaningful, compelling and consist manner is one of the Entrepreneur's most necessary skills.*

The ability to pitch, i.e., to get your key message across in a meaningful, compelling, and concise manner, is one of the Entrepreneur's most necessary skill sets. It is remarkable then, that it is also one of the skills most often missing.

W. Daniel Mothersill, President of the National Angel Organization, Pitch Coach for the Toronto Venture Group, Chair of the Ciris Group of Companies, and one of the key voices at Ernst & Young's cross country Entrepreneurial Bootcamp program, puts it this way:

> *"Most pitches are about as exciting as a bowl of cold oatmeal, but not as good for the digestion. For the most part, these quick pitches can best be categorized as trite, trivial, and tepid. Too often they devolve into warmed-over motherhood statements, weighted down by techno-speak and spiced with jargon."*

In meeting with over 2,000 entrepreneurs at over 70-plus bootcamps, Mothersill states that pitching is where most of the attendees come up short.

"They make these disembodied statements sort of describing what their company does, but they almost never talk about the market pain it solves. They miss the whole point," said Mothersill.

"No pain, no gain must be the mantra for anyone creating an elevator pitch. In a few short sentences, you need to tie in your audience's needs, wants, and desires directly to your company's offerings. I've helped a couple of thousand companies to do this. It can take as much as a day to develop, but yields dividends for a lifetime."

So how do you create a powerful elevator pitch? Well, first you need to understand exactly what an "Elevator Pitch" is and where it comes from.

Where Does The Term Elevator Pitch Come From?

I first heard the term Elevator Pitch when I worked in New York during the dot.com boom. I'm sure it dates back much farther, but during the boom, Elevator Pitching was elevated (no pun intended) to the status of urban legend. So, where does the name come from?

As told to me, the legend suggested that entrepreneurs seeking capital would lurk in the office lobby of investors, quietly awaiting the arrival of their target – the Venture Capitalist. Then, once said VC arrived, the skulking entrepreneur (preferably skulking only in spirit), would follow the VC onto the elevator. Once the doors had closed, the founders would whip out a binder containing a few slides and pitch the investor their idea. These harried founders had only a few moments to pitch their ideas; for once the VC reached their office floor, one of two things would happen: the investor would invite them into the board room to hear more; or the investor would call security (literal skulkers having been apprehended long ago in the lobby).

And from this, the term and the legend of the Elevator Pitch was born.

Even though the bubble has long since burst, the Elevator Pitch parable still rings true today. When it comes to pitching, you need to envision yourself in an elevator with your target audience, knowing that you only have a few floors to capture their attention, build credibility, and more importantly leave them craving for more.

What Is An Elevator Pitch?

VCexperts.com defines an Elevator Pitch as: An extremely concise presentation of an entrepreneur's idea, business model, company solution, marketing strategy, and competition delivered to potential investors. It should not last more than a few minutes, or the duration of an elevator ride.

The MIT Enterprise Forum defines an Elevator Pitch as: "A one minute description of a company designed to encourage the audience to become investors, employees, or customers"

At the Bootcamps, Dan and I, define an Elevator Pitch as: A clear, concise, compelling combination of the pain your venture is addressing and the value proposition your business is providing.

Why Is The Elevator Pitch So Important?

VCs, like all investors, see hundreds of investment opportunities a year. So how does one make sure their venture gets the attention it deserves? You guessed it – the Elevator Pitch.

According to Salim Teja, Vice-President with Brightspark Ventures, one of the few true seed investors left in Canada, the Elevator Pitch is not just a simple introduction to an idea. He explains that: *"The difference between good meetings and bad meetings with investors is the first five minutes. This is the entrepreneur's chance to clearly communicate their vision, passion and expertise. The ability to deliver a well-crafted Elevator Pitch sets the tone for the entire meeting."*

As Teja puts it, good pitching is usually a sign that not only does management understand the heart of their business, but they are also effective communicators.

"The ability to convey a concise and compelling pitch showcases the vision of the entrepreneur. This ability to focus strengthens the investor's confidence in the team and provides added assurance that management will be able to turn its vision into an appropriate operating plan," said Teja. *"Conversely, I'd have a hard time getting behind a*

founder that lacks the ability to get me interested in what he does in under a minute."

What's The Secret Of The Elevator Pitch?

Kerri Knull, a reformed venture capitalist, now manager of the Financing Your Vision programs for Calgary Technologies Inc. (a not for profit Alberta incubator that helps Western companies succeed), tells me that: *"The secret to the perfect elevator pitch lies in your ability to briefly and clearly articulate how your product will improve your customer's life and why they cannot live another day without it. If you can distill your message down to just a few powerful sentences, you strengthen investor confidence in your team's talent for developing a sharp vision and executing on the business plan."*

This is something that I wholeheartedly agree with. You have to focus on and start with the pain. After all, if there is no pain, what is the need for your solution? The size of the pain is a key ingredient used by investors when determining the true size of an investment opportunity.

Size Of Opportunity = Size Of The Market x Size Of Pain

The size of the opportunity is thus dependent on two factors: the number of people succumbing to the pain regularly and the cost of the pain. To be truly persuasive you must therefore disobey your mother (this one time) and "BE A BIG PAIN". The bigger the pain, the more compelling the need for your solution, and consequently the more investors will want to learn more.

How To Write The Elevator Pitch?

There are six key steps to crafting a solid elevator pitch:

1. Put your end user hat on to find the why:

Start creating your Elevator Pitch by first putting yourself in the shoes of your clients. What is it that compels them to spend money with you? Not what do they buy, but why do they buy it. Imagine polling your end user base and asking them "what is it you are suffering from?" and "what is the one thing that causes you the most pain?

2. Quantify that pain to establish credibility:

No one ever came into my offices trumpeting a "lukewarm" idea. To them it is invariably "the greatest idea ever." Subsequently, like most venture capitalists, I immediately want to know who else thinks that what they are doing is the greatest or most necessary? But most of all, I want to know who else believes it to be monetize-able?

Third-part credibility is always necessary, even in your Elevator Pitch. Find a number that can be validated and works in your favour – then incorporate it into your pitch. For example:

- How many people suffer from the problem you are solving?

- How much money is spent currently solving that problem?

- Who else (besides you), believes that this issue must be addressed?

3. Develop a hook to grab their attention:

Combine the results of steps 1 and 2 into a hook to pull listeners in. Make sure that the hook is irrefutable. After all, you don't want your audience to challenge you before you even finish the opening line of your pitch

.

4. Describe your Value Proposition:

Combining steps 1, 2 & 3 to create one half of the Elevator Pitch – the Pain Statement. Next, you must shift your attention from the pain to the solution, aka the Value Proposition. From the start, it is key to bluntly and efficiently tell your audience "what you do." Nothing irks an investor more than having to wait to determine what a company actually does to make money. So make sure that you start the second half of your Elevator Pitch by letting them know what you do - not with techno-babble, but with a clear concise phrase, e.g. *We build software that powers the financial engines of stock markets.*

5. Focus on the key benefits:

Everyone has competition; that much is true no matter what your venture. But seldom do you get to choose the competitive factors on which your venture will be judged. Is a Volvo better than a Porsche, or vice versa? Well, frankly that all depends on which criteria you use. If safety is your main concern, then the Volvo might be perceived as the better car. However, if speed is the deciding factor, the Porsche will most likely be seen as the better choice.

Use the second part of the Elevator Pitch – the Value Proposition, to set the tone for the key criteria that you feel your customers demand. Focus on the benefits most important to your client when writing the Value Statement and do so in a manner that positions you strongly against those key criteria while describing them from a customer's perspective.

This is also where tag lines may come in. A tagline is sometimes a subset or variation of the Value Proposition, and can often help in setting the tone for the Elevator Pitch's second half. You need to go no further than the old standard created by Timex years ago. The Timex tagline *"Takes a Licking and Keeps on Ticking"* shows that durability is the key benefit Timex feels their clients are seeking. What's your venture's tagline?

6. Put it together and test it (often):

Putting the above together generates the key equation behind the Elevator Pitch:

Elevator Pitch = Pain Statement + Value Proposition

But once you have satisfied this equation you need to test it and I highly recommend twofold testing.

First, prove your new pitch against the four factors that every Elevator Pitch must meet:

1. Irrefutable – Can someone argue against your pitch right away or does it pass the "smell test." Nothing is worse than giving your pitch and before you can move on, the listener says "I don't agree." Elevator Pitches must be, on their face, irrefutable at first blush.

2. Easily Understandable – Can both your six year old daughter and your seventy-three year old grandfather understand your pitch? Do they get what you do based on only the pitch? If not, start again. You must ensure that you don't include any techie talk, acronyms or other confusing statements. Everyone no matter their age, experience or background must "get" what you are pitching the first time.

3. Succinct – Remember, you only have a "few floors" to give your Elevator Pitch, so keep it under a minute – preferably under half a minute.

4. Greed Inducing – Your proverbial goal is to get invited off the elevator and into the board room. Your pitch must therefore compel a listener to demand that you tell them more. It must be viewed as a call to action. In the case of most pitch audiences (investors, clients and employees) it must induce greed. Hence you must always ensure your pitch leaves the audience with a feeling that being involved with the venture will make or save them money. After all, for a commercial audience, this is what it is all about.

Second, practice your pitch - A LOT! Recruit family, friends, employees, etc. and pitch in front of them again and again. Ask them to listen to your Elevator pitch, and then see if they can answer these key questions:

- What do we do for a living?

- What problem are we solving?

- What is the primary benefit of our solution? And who benefits?

- Why would our customers buy?

- Would you want to hear more?

You will want to continue to refine your Elevator Pitch until all of your audience can answer the above questions correctly. Some imaginary examples:

- Millions of people want to have sex longer than their bodies will allow. Our blue, aspirin-sized, FDA approved tablet allows them to do so in a cost effective, non-evasive manner...**Viagra**

- One Man's trash is another man's treasure. Our online e-marketplace moves garage sales from your front lawn to the global marketplace allowing millions of people to bid on the goods you no longer need but can't be bothered to sell and allowing millions of people to find that missing item from their treasured collection that they can't find locally...**Ebay**

- Smaller and lighter than any CD player, our 21st century mobile digital jukebox can hold thousands of songs digitally allowing you to take them wherever you go and providing you with more than 10x the capacity for entertainment...**iPod**

The Bottom Line

You only get one chance to make a first impression, so make sure it counts. Continue to craft your Elevator Pitch until you have something that is succinct, irrefutable, accessible and greed inducing. Ensure that your final Elevator Pitch is something that every member of your organization can adopt and incorporate into every pitch, whether it is for new capital, new partnerships or new talent. Remember – in today's world, the entrepreneur's mantra needs to be *Clamo, ergo sum* (I pitch, therefore I am).

Chapter 7

What A VC Wants

Originally Published March 15, 2006

In the 2000 romantic comedy *What Women Want*, Mel Gibson gains the ability to hear women's thoughts. His new found ability yields insight into an enigmatic world and expands his previously limited horizons.

In the last 30 days, I have been approached to raise Venture Capital on behalf of many ventures, including a dog treat manufacturer, a new toilet seat cover designer and an on-line simulated hockey league. After listening to their pitches it was clear to me, that like Mel Gibson who struggled to gain insight into the mysterious minds of women, some people are often stuck in an abyss when trying to understand the minds of Venture Capitalists.

While I doubt that I will ever truly gain, let alone be able to share with you, insight on Mel's discovery, I was able to touch base with five very different venture capitalists and ask their opinion on what VCs consider fundamental when (or before) making an investment. Even though each VC investor comes from different parts of the world and each focuses on very different sectors and stages of investment, they more or less independently came up with the same five core elements that get them excited about a deal. So while I can't shed any light on what women want, I may be able to illuminate what most VCs need before even considering an investment.

1. A Large opportunity

As discussed in previous articles, the size of opportunity (a.k.a. the total addressable market) can be calculated, as the size of the pain multiplied by the quantity of customers experiencing that pain. Experienced VCs know that your venture is most likely only going to get a modest market penetration at least at first and hence, they figure that you are only going to pick up at best a small portion of the total addressable market. Therefore, your company will need to have a large enough total market, to make even the smallest segment valuable. This is why you need an expansive market with a large pain to attract VC funding.

"Size of market is key. Within the next 3-5 years the market that the venture is going to sell into must show a demand of at least half a billion with double-digit CAGR [Compound Annual Growth Rate]," says Larry Lam, from BDC Venture Capital. However, the overall size of the market isn't as important as the pent up demand or the pain that needs to be addressed. *"The product must create value for the customer, they must really want it. It either needs to solve a big problem they have or lead to some better state in the near future,"* adds Les Lyall, Senior Vice-President at Growthworks, whose funds invest in almost all sectors and stages.

The ability to gain traction and the need to scale (see #4) all increase the likelihood of generating a high exit value (#5). All three of these items are dependent on the high (or expressed) demand for your product. The market or pain cannot merely exist. It is imperative that the market be big enough that the people struggling with a problem will be inclined to pay for a (or the) solution.

As an example, let's use e-mail spam fighting software. We have all received thousands of unwanted email advertising, with subject headlines such as body enlarging herbs and get rich schemes (among others). How much would you pay to clear your inbox of these unwanted messages? Now think of how much Corporate America would pay. In 2004 the cost of spam to Corporate America was over $21B, reflective of a market with a large pain.

2. Strong Competitive Advantage

It is not enough to simply target a market with a large pain. Once you have begun dominating your addressable market, you must be able to defend (or secure) that territory.

Competition comes in many forms, including direct, indirect, alternatives, and of course the one that most start-ups never think about, *Status Quo*. But assuming the pain is big enough (see #1), then the status quo menace or the "we are fine the way we are, so we don't need to buy your product" is mitigated; you will still need to address your competition.

If anyone can easily replicate what you are doing, then you are likely to face two large sources of competitive pressure. The first one comes from other startups and incumbents. It will not sit well with investors if others can easily pursue a venture that is similar to yours. The second comes from the "buy vs. build" decision. If your future clients feel that the product, while good isn't very hard to build, they might decide to simply create their own version internally and leave yours on the store shelf. Regardless of the type of competitive pressure confronting your new venture, it can have devastating effects.

This is often why VCs want intellectual property, especially with early stage companies who don't yet have deep relationships with customers. Investors want affirmation that once the product receives traction, you can defend your hard fought market share, not only because your venture has the best solution to the customer's problem, but because your IP locks out others.

IP is also important when it comes to achieving a high exit value (#5). If you are able to lock other solutions out of the market with your **IP,** then it is more likely you will be acquired by those wishing to sell into your customer base, since they can't build it themselves; they either need to license it from you, or buy you outright.

Revisiting the spam situation, a company that has a patented solution to block spam in a novel way more accurately than any other solution, will more likely find itself in the M&A sights of vendors, who sell email solutions to Corporate America. If the future acquirer can simply build a similar system, then the value proposition for acquisition drops dramatically.

But not all investors think IP is the strongest barrier to entry. Kevin Effusy, a Partner in the Silicon Valley based Accel Partners, who focuses on wireless, software and Web 2.0 ventures, expresses that while IP is nice to have, nothing beats customer traction. More specifically, he states that *"The network effect (e.g. the service becomes stronger as more users sign up) and building pervasive technology (a platform upon which others build, making it harder to later replace the underlying platform) can be huge competi-*

tive advantages" and can likewise act as strong barriers to entry. One has only to look to Skype, eBay or Facebook, to see the former or JBoss and Microsoft to witness the latter.

Notwithstanding, it is less important where your strong competitive advantage and barriers to entry come from; all that matters is that you have them.

3. Management

Salim Teja, Vice-president with BrightSpark Ventures, a seed investor focusing on Software, says *"Sixty per cent of the investment decision comes down to the quality of management. Amongst other things, we look for founders with deep technical expertise. Bring us the best in the world in his area, and we'll be interested. It is not enough to just be a bit better though. Today, to win clients, you need to be exponentially better and to do that you need deep technical expertise on your team."*

Most investors agree that a brilliant technologist is needed for the team, since it is technology that often produces the competitive advantage (see #2) but technical knowledge is only one part of the management equation. According to Benoit Hogue, from Montreal based Propulsion Ventures, many VCs also like to bet on founders with extensive domain knowledge. *"Management is our first criteria and we measure quality along two key axes: one - deep domain expertise and two - the killer instinct to succeed"* says Hogue. *"We want someone who understands the customers pain (#1) and will ensure the solution being built*

> **Wise Words # 10**
> *Sixty per cent of the investment decision comes down to the quality of Management.*

addresses such. Otherwise you can end up with good technology that simply won't sell."

Killer instinct was also important to David Raffa, a Partner with BC Advantage Funds, an early stage VC on the West Coast. Raffa says *"Venture capital is all about three things: people, people, people. I look for a bright, cohesive A level team that simply will not be denied. No matter how smart you think you are, or how great your technology is, you are going to face both expected and unexpected challenges. How the team responds to those challenges will be the difference between a good idea that dies, and a good idea that goes on to become a great one."*

Once again, let's reflect on our e-mail spam example. Do you think it is more important to understand the mind of the Corporate CIO who will potentially buy the product or simply build the best technologically sound spam blocker? The answer is neither. Ideally, VCs want to invest in management teams that can do both and do so with that "we won't be denied" attitude.

4. The Ability To Scale

In a nutshell, to be scalable from a VC's perspective, means that as you roll out your product, the costs associated with it do not increase in lock-step with the revenues. On-line software businesses are extremely scalable. Once you have built the first unit, the costs have sunk and you need not rebuild the product to sell it again. Conversely, consulting businesses are not very scalable. Increasing revenues necessitate a larger staff, billing more hours or selling at a higher price, all of which may be feasibly capped as you roll out your solution. This is why VCs typically don't invest in consulting businesses, IT outsourcing companies or ventures that are purely service oriented; they simply don't scale.

"We look for companies that can conceivably be grown to a large size quickly while maintaining, or better yet increasing, profit margins," says Les Lyall. Benoit agrees that *"VC money is the wrong medicine if you can't scale. There is nothing wrong with a business doing $10M in revenues with $1M in profits. In fact, I'd quit my job to own one, but if that is as big as it can get, that's not for VC investors."*

5. The Potential For A High Exit

Raffa comments that *"A logical buyer needs to be self evident ... although in the end, some deals get done with buyers you wouldn't necessarily think of. However, as an investor, on day one, you want to be able to say to yourself, "Yeah, I can see who will buy this company and why. The next step then is to determine for how much and when."*

After five-to-seven years (the typical fund life cycle), most VCs typically seek to get out 5-1x the amount they invested. This is why most institutional investors only seriously consider companies that can hit $50M + in revenue in short order. They know that most tech acquisitions are done as a multiple of revenue. Therefore, if they have invested $5M and own 30% of the company at exit, they need to have the company selling $50M + in product annually and still get at least a multiple of 2x on sale. This is why scaling (see item #4) into a large market (#1), is so important to venture capitalists.

Lyall agrees with Raffa on this point. *"There needs to be potential exits. There have to be companies or public share-holders who will buy the company once it's built and scaled. Ideally, there would be companies who would want to acquire the venture for strategic reasons".* Hence there is the need for a strong competitive advantage (#2)

Lyall corroborates this by suggesting, that, "If the buyer needs that venture's product to stay in business or grow, you are most likely going to get a better price for it."

The Bottom Line

As I tend to fall asleep during romantic comedies, I'm at a loss to tell you how Mel's movie ended; however, I do hope that the above has helped you peer into the mysterious minds of venture capitalists. Now all that remains is one final question: Do you need to have all five of these "prerequisites" in place before you go seeking investment?

The answer; not by a long shot. As Propulsion's Hogue states, *"If you are weak in one area, it is fine, just make sure you are off the charts in the other areas to compensate."* A sentiment that Accel's Effusy agrees with but puts another way: *"Quite frankly, it is rare that all five of these items are present in the same company in the beginning. You typically start with one or two elements that are extraordinary and that you believe in deeply and then you have to make a leap of faith. After all that is why they call it Venture Capital".*

Notwithstanding, all the parties surveyed agreed that the stronger you are in each of the 5 elements, the more likely it is that "what VCs want" will be to invest in you.

Chapter 8

The Direct V. Channel Sales Debate

Originally published August 18, 2006

There is a famous maxim that says *"The shortest distance between two points is a straight line"* and while no doubt a truism, the shortest distance is not always the best route to take. The same can be said for sales rollouts with regard to the decision between building an internal sales force, and leveraging a pre-existing group of resellers.

Every entrepreneur dreams of the day when their sales rocket up from $500,000 to $35,000,000. Along the way however, every entrepreneur is faced with a key strategic sales decision: ramping up firm sales by building an internal sales force (the Direct Sales Model), v. leveraging third-party market intermediaries to sell on your behalf (the Channel Sales Model). In pondering this decision, founders need to ask themselves several key questions, including:

- On what criteria should you base that decision?
- When does one approach beat the other?
- If I choose one, do I have to stick with it, or does it evolve over time?
- When do you need to make that decision?

To tackle some of these issues, I sat down with Les Hansen, Vice-President of Sales & Marketing for Gavel & Grown Software, a venture capital-backed software firm selling enterprise solutions to the legal profession. Since joining Gavel & Gown, Les has managed to sell more than 250,000 licenses through a well-managed sales and distribution program which leverages both a small dedicated internal sales team, and a small army of resellers around the globe. Les shared with me "The 5 C's" – which he believes entrepreneurs need to consider when pondering the Direct v. Channel sales decision.

Cost: What's The Best Way To Spend Your Money?

The cost of building a direct sales force internally can be daunting. Not only do you have to hire, train, and support them, you also have to allocate additional funds for draws, employee benefits, and sales support. In addition, you must do all of this before a single unit of product is sold. Giving up a percentage of future sales revenue in the form of reseller margin may seem cheap in comparison, but *"you must think this is through,"* cautions Hansen. *"You need to first calculate the breakeven point on the direct cost of a sales force vs. the margin cost of the channel,"* says this experienced sales strategist. *"Remember that, for the most part, direct sales costs are fixed (apart from the commission component), and channel costs are variable. This also means that direct sales costs can be leveraged while channel margins costs cannot."*

In this way, you need to be able to look at the long-term picture; seeing not only the short-term sales costs, but also the long-term revenue potential. You also need to allocate fixed costs to areas where you can get the highest ROI. It is in those areas where you get the most bang for your buck. R&D into new products is a must. So, you have to ask yourself: should I allocate salary to more developers, or to more internal sales people? You can scale the returns on the R&D team much better, so that may be a better place to spend your employee dollars.

Customer: How Much Customer Interaction Do You Need?

Finding a customer that is willing to buy is hard. Building a relationship that will ensure they continue to buy – much more so. Channel partners provide your venture with a much larger reach, but you need to balance the channel's ability to leverage pre-existing relationships, with your need to access direct customer feedback – especially in the early days of product development and beta testing, when customer feedback is vital to ensure long-term viability of the product. However, in the end, you need to weigh the long-term impact of keeping your customers at arms' length v. the ability to have a larger number of feet on the street hawking your product.

Calendar: How Long Do You Have?

Building an internal sales force takes time. Even once you have them hired and trained and raring to go, it will take still more time for them to go out, meet customers, qualify targets, build leverage-able relationships, and establish enough customer credibility to actually close a sale. Do you as a start-up have that much time, or do you need to leverage a channel that is already selling similar products to your target audience?

Investors want scalability (the ability to ramp up revenue fast, and to do so without proportionately ramping up costs) and maximizing scalability often means deploying a channel sales force.

"Without those extra feet on the street, most VC's will have a lot harder time believing in a venture's ability to scale up to $35M+ in 3-

5 years. It just takes too long to scale up internally, and without scalability, the VC will have a hard time getting their head around an investment," confirms Phil Reddon, a VP with Covington Capital, a venture capital fund with more than $500 million under management.

Complexity: How Complicated Is The Product?

The more complex the product is, the harder it will be to drive sales through a channel, or so one might think. *"There's a myth out there that if your product is complex, you have to sell it direct. But that simply isn't an absolute truth,"* says Hansen. "In many cases, when the product is complex, you need channel partners to not only sell the product, but also to integrate the product into the client's existing infrastructure, to service and update the product on an ongoing basis and to provide end-user training on functionality."

This makes sense to me; as a direct sales force, which just makes commissions on moving sales units, may not focus on after-sale support. *"In complex sales, you may need your channel to not only sell your product, but to also sell additional products and services that, when packaged with your product, create a complete solution offering for the customer,"* Les shares: *"This can be a real advantage for you. Many channel resellers will make 5-10x as much money on the consulting services they sell alongside your product as they do on the margin you give them. This means that they will have significant incentive to sell your product, and it can save you margin dollars. It also allows you to focus on your core competency. If you are not an integrator you shouldn't try to be one. You should partner with someone who is."*

Control: Who Owns The Customer?

Another key sales maxim is: "He who is closest to the customer owns the customer." This means that down the road, your channel partners may own your customers and therefore, if they walk, so may some of your customers. So you need to consider the impact of this. Is this a business risk that you can live with? While customer poaching does happen when internal sales reps switch to a competing firm, the terms of most employment contracts can mitigate this significantly. Accept that you will have much less control over your channel partners than you would over a direct sales force, which can be a challenge. Will you be able to exert enough influence over your channel partners to comfortably achieve your business objectives? If not, can you live with this?

Control also addresses your ability to make adjustments on the fly and to influence the sales messaging quickly when needed, according to Hansen. *"In start-up software sales, you may not get your go to Market plan and message perfect right out of the gate, so you need to be flexible and be able to respond quickly. It is a lot easier to control your external communication through a sales team that reports directly to you, than through a channel with which you have an arms' length relationship. Managing a message through a channel can sometimes be a lot like that game 'broken telephone'. You need to be concise and clear, or the message may get distorted as it disseminates."*

So, there you have it, "Hansen's 5 C's" – which outline the key matters you should consider before choosing a go to market strategy; but what about the timing of the decision?

Evolving The Approach

In the venture capital world, where scalability and rapid growth are prerequisites for investment, the channel sales model seems to be preferred. *"From a VC perspective, I like to see a company which can leverage other people's sales forces to grow. Yes, your company will give up some points in margin and also lose some control over customer relationships, but will hopefully make up for it in terms of more volume,"* posts Ed Sim, Managing Director at New York City's Dawntrender Ventures, in his blog *BEYOND VC.*

Stephen Pollack, CEO of the Toronto based venture backed PlateSpin and an IT Veteran with a wealth of experience in creating and delivering software and software service, agrees with SIM: *"We found that establishing a global business model was only possible through a channel approach. That was a main driver for us along with the desire to work through trusted sources (that) the customer can rely on instead of a "startup in some far away place'. We now have 1000 customers spread all over the world through our channel model"*

Therefore, if you decide on building channels, the question then becomes when to focus on such. Covington's Reddon comments: *"Companies need to land, usually via direct-initiatives, commercial reference-able customers first. Then once they have enough proof of concept installs, they can turn to channelizing the process."* Mike Green, President, Greenco Investments Corp. (and former Chair of the Toronto Angel Group who now works closely with several young software companies on issues including sales rollouts), echoes this notion: *"There is no point in moving to an indirect channel until AFTER you have got it right with your own direct sales efforts. Once you understand what it takes to sell ... can communicate the typical sales cycle, your key selling points, and ...*
60

handle the standard sales objections, then you are ready to give the in-direct sales channel the ammunition they need to be successful...but not before!"

Tips For Managing Channel Sales

Once you've got the ammunition and information from those first 20+ reference-able customers, you are ready to start building out your channels. To do this, Hansen says that the fastest way is to find a group of like-minded individuals who are already in deep with your target customer base. The best way to do that? *"Ride someone else's channel. Never build when you can borrow,"* Hansen comments. *"Take a look at the products that your target customers are already buying, and find out who they're buying them from. Chances are that someone has an established distribution channel into the market segment you want to get to."* Remember – if you have a product and are looking for a channel, somebody out there probably has a channel and they are looking to push more products through that existing channel. Even better – if you can establish integration between your product and theirs, you can improve the revenue generating capability of single sales call, allowing the sales reps to 'double-dip' their commissions.

However, channel management does not end there. Once you have the channel, you not only need to maintain it – you need to motivate it. Hansen gives three pieces of advice to future channel managers: "Be fair – your channel partners expect it. Be consistent – your channel partners will talk to each other, so accept it. Be friendly – relationships go a long way, so invest in them."

The Bottom Line

There are definitely pros and cons on both sides of the Direct v. Channel debate. A direct sales force allows you more customer interactivity, but may cost more (in terms of both time and money). Harnessing a channel sales approach allows you to leverage on pre-existing relationships, but does not offer up as much control. Neither model is perfect, nor can either be applied in all cases. The shortest distance between two points may be a straight line, but the shortest distance is not the only route to take - and it certainly is not the best route to pursue under all circumstances.

Chapter 9

The Talent Triangle

Originally published May 17, 2006

"We like to bet on the jockey not the horse"

"I'll always back an A team with a B opportunity over a B team with an A opportunity",

"In Real Estate it is LOCATION, LOCATION. LOCATION. In investing it is MANAGEMENT, MANAGEMENT. MANAGEMENT."

These are only a few of the axioms common to the venture and angel investment landscape that stress the important role management plays in the investment decision process. This management bias was confirmed a few years ago in a survey produced by the National Venture Capital Association ("NVCA"). The members of the NVCA considered management, as the most heavily weighted factor when deciding to invest in a particular venture (i.e. management received over 35 per cent of the weight, compared with 25 per cent, 20 per cent and 15 per cent for the market opportunity/sector, business model and the actual technology/product respectively). This of course assists in answering the question, "What factor do investors put the most weight on when reviewing an opportunity?' What it does not answer, however, is "What do investors look for when evaluating management?" After straw polling some colleagues on this question, most of my VC peers share the NVCA's findings, but felt that the 35 per cent figure may even be too low (one colleague stated he based as much as 60 per cent of the investment decision on the quality of management). The answer most frequently offered was "we look for a well-rounded team that can increase the probability of the venture's success." In response to this answer, I ask, what defines a "well rounded team that can increase the probability of a venture's success?" In order to satisfy my query, I delved into the archives.

A few years ago, when I was working for Ernst & Young's Venture Capital Group, I decided to investigate what a well-rounded management team consisted of, by issuing a survey to 500 of the most successful high-growth companies (based on multiple year published lists of the Profit 100, Deloitte's Fast 50 and Ernst & Young's Entrepreneur of the Year program winners). The goal of the survey was to determine if there were common management elements among the high-growth companies. The results showed that more than 80 per cent of the successful high-growth companies had common management elements.

> **Wise Words # 11**
> *Domain knowledge, vision and passion are critical to a startup, but nothing is ever sold without a sales guy.*

Based on this survey, the attributes of a successful management team included three key elements: business acumen, operational experience and domain knowledge. These elements form the corners of what we coined, the "Talent Triangle." In addition, the survey revealed that having the right cogs in place was vital, but even more important was how those cogs interacted with each other.

A management team with all three elements, should structure its business to ensure that each segment of the triangle, has not only the responsibility for its own portfolio, but also the authority to make decisions on issues under its specific jurisdiction. We called this strategy, "The BODCAT Decision-Making Model".

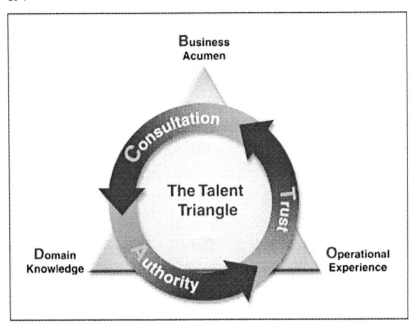

Figure 1: **The BODCAT Management Model**

The BODCAT Management Model refers to the three key elements of the Talent Triangle, which again include, business acumen, operational experience and domain knowledge. Consultation, authority and trust, facilitate the decision making process. To help illustrate this, I will use a hypothetical startup that sells automobiles on-line to the general public, Ab-leAuto.com.

Element 1: Business Acumen

A person with Business Acumen is most often seen carrying the title CEO, President or CFO, because he or she has the skill, knowledge and experience to make key business decisions. These people are focused on HR management, investor relations and overall corporate development, which are all consistent with their expertise in venture evolution. The person in the Business Acumen corner of the Talent Triangle is often responsible for ensuring that the venture focuses only on core competencies that add direct value to their startup. They might have 20 years of professional services experience or experience in running a business and although they might lack domain expertise, they **must** have the ability to make top-level decisions that encourage the company's growth. Similarly, a person with business acumen, must be a strong communicator and able to assume a leadership role. Sam Znaimer, Senior VP from Ventures West put it this way;

"Domain knowledge, vision, and passion are critical to a startup, but nothing is ever sold without a sales guy cementing a relationship or pushing for a close. Whether it's selling product to end users, distribution relationships to channel partners, or stock to venture capitalists, the core of the team must include a communicator who can command unreasonable loyalty and close the deal."

As an interesting aside, one of the qualitative comments generated by the survey suggested that you must line up the type of business acumen the CFO has, with the stage of the business.

For instance, a CEO with years of public-company experience might not have the ability to lead a startup venture. If we look to AbleAuto.com, the business acumen leader requires startup experience, but not necessarily startup experience in the car business or even in on-line selling. Larry Marcus, from the California based fund, Walden VC, corroborates this finding by stating, that *"Companies at different stages require different skill-sets. Management needs to evolve. Early on, it takes more domain knowledge and product focus. Later, it shifts, [and the question then becomes]"can you bring it to market, and do you have the business acumen to scale up and respond to customers' needs and growth?"*

Element 2: Operational Experience

According to Rick Segal, Partner with JL Albright Ventures, "ops," is the key to a strong fundable team. He comments that, *"The most important part of management is operational experience. The ability to understand the issues, feel the pain and know in your gut what to do, often times will carry the day."*

People with ops experience are focused on infrastructure, logistics, and most importantly, product development. These founders often carry the title, COO, CTO, or VP of R&D and occupy the Operations Experience corner of the Talent Triangle. Their job is to make decisions that relate to the venture's implementation and execution of its business plan. They not only build what the startup will sell, but they are also responsible for making sure it is shipped and supported. These people need hands-on experience in technical product development, setting up delivery chains, inventory management, and selecting and managing outsourced partners. I think that Roger Wilson, of Toronto's BDC Venture Capital software group, put it best when he articulated that, *"Once the initial code to the Company's positioning,*

67

messaging and pitch to the outside world has been "cracked," increased attention must be turned more inwardly to operational processes to allow the Company to scale in areas including: customer support, implementation, sales, ongoing product development/innovation, etc. This ensures that, while the Company continues to delight more and more customers, over time, it does so increasingly through an efficient and highly profitable business model."

In AbleAuto.com, the operational experience corner is not only charged with designing the website from which the customers order their cars, but they are also responsible for choosing the 1SP host, co-ordinating the delivery of vehicles sold on the site, and managing security in the data chain.

Element 3: Domain Knowledge

The individual who brings Domain Knowledge to the team must understand the industry's key value motivators, be aware of the domain's impediments to ensure that the supply chain is not interrupted and possess the necessary relationships in the market to make sales. Domain Knowledge experts often have business cards that read, VP Sales, VP Business Development or Director of Corporate Development. The Domain Knowledge expert, **must** have years of hands-on experience in the target industry, even if it is from a "big company" perspective. It is this person's job to ensure that the startup's product and value proposition meet and possibly exceed the needs of end-users.

In-depth knowledge of the car market, as well as an understanding of the relationships between automobile manufacturers, their dealer network, and the car-buying public, are necessary requirements for the Domain Knowledge leader of AbleAuto.com. Domain experts are responsible for making the first and by far the most important sales – the reference accounts (a/k/a beachhead accounts). Marc Faucher, from BCE Capital- describes it this way: *"Deep domain knowledge, specifically a strong network of contacts into potential target customers, is arguably THE most important component of a well-rounded management team. Securing that beachhead account is pivotal for any early stage company. One's ability to accelerate that process by leaning on existing relationships, in my opinion, is invaluable."*

What Happens If One Of The Elements Is Missing?

While the survey shows that all three elements of the Talent Triangle must be present for a balanced management team and for the highest probability of success, it is worth noting that in most cases you do not need 3 people (i.e. one person in each corner). The founders of Microsoft, Dell and Google occupied multiple corners simultaneously. Therefore, although our survey found that the Talent Triangle was typically covered by 4-5 members of the management team, it is less about the quantity and all about the quality. Notwithstanding, without all three corners, the triangle ceases to exist and the venture lacks the prerequisites for rapid growth.

The absence of any one of the three major components of the Talent Triangle might create a monumental void that, while not necessarily causing the failure of the startup, will definitely hinder the company's ability to raise venture capital and limit the number of interested investors. To expand on this, we shall consider the following scenarios:

- A business that has Business Acumen and Operational Experience, but lacks Domain Knowledge, might create a well-run venture with an excellent website and delivery model, but will achieve minimal sales or develop a less-than-attractive product based on low client interactivity.

- A startup with strong Business Acumen and extensive Domain Knowledge, but insufficient Operational Experience, might offer investors a venture with a good product and lean infrastructure, but lacks the efficacy to execute and fulfill sales.

- A company with Operational Experience and Domain Knowledge that lacks the necessary Business Acumen might end up with a great product and efficient delivery methods, but it will also have a bloated infrastructure, high staff turnover and larger-out burn rates than necessary.

So what is the bottom line you ask? While Angels, seed investors and friends and family might be willing to support a management team without the necessary three elements, it is less than likely that traditional venture capitalists will. With this said, all investors look to mitigate risk in three key areas: magic (will the product work?), market (will anyone buy it?) and management (can they create a viable company?).

Decision-making in the Talent Triangle

Simply having all three elements in the team is not enough. To maximize the probability of success, a venture must coat the Talent Triangle with a properly balanced effective decision-making process. The BODCAT Decision-Making Model does this by encompassing three elements:

(1) Consultation: Decisions are made in consultation amongst all three elements and wherever possible, consensus is sought. This increases the probability that decisions will be sound, not only

from a business perspective, but also from an industry standpoint. Similarly, it ensures that decisions are efficiently executed.

(2) Authority: Each member of the Talent Triangle should not only have the responsibility for making decisions that fall within his or her own area of expertise, but should also reserve the authority to make the final call if consensus cannot be reached. Responsibility without authority will lead to frustration and substandard decisions.

(3) Trust: Management teams must at all times strive for internal agreement. Each member of the management team, must therefore, implicitly trust all partners, so that whenever consensus cannot be reached and a final decision is made, the other members of the team offer their energy and support for the decision. External parties such as VCs, clients, and suppliers must always believe that a venture's management team is in 100% agreement. Divide and conquer is an old investor trick. To prevent this, make sure that every member of the team is always singing from the same song sheet, even if they were originally not in agreement with the tune.

The best illustration for the need to deploy the BODCAT management model comes from the 2001 MTV documentary. *Startup.com.* This unique look at the rise and fall of a startup in the late 90's showed the damage that can arise when management does not employ consultation, authority and trust. What starts off as a potential homerun, strikes out as the founders' relationship implodes.

The Bottom Line

There is no quick answer as to why some startups fail, while others succeed. Industry conditions, price fluctuations, consumer tastes and a host of other external factors all affect a venture's bottom line and are generally outside management's sphere of influence. You can however, improve your odds by ensuring that all three elements of the Talent Triangle are in place and by putting The BODCAT Decision-Making Model to good use. This will provide your management team with a solid foothold and increase your venture's overall chance of success, not only at raising venture capital, but at creating a truly viable high-growth startup.

Chapter 10

The Cup, The Wallet & The Sword:

How Starting A Business Is Like Starting A Family, And How To Choose Your Partner For Either

Originally published June 16, 2006

As you may have realized by now, I often employ unconventional wisdom when trying to mentor entrepreneurs and startups. A few years ago, I went to listen to a Rabbi from New York. His lecture topic, entitled, *How To Choose A Partner For Life?* got me thinking. I wondered if his advice for finding a life mate could be applied similarly when in search for a business partner. After much thought, I concluded that starting a family is much like starting a business and as such, the recommended criteria for a successful personal union is as valid for a business partnership.

Are they the same?

Is starting a family the same as starting a company? Both endeavors require hard work, open communication, shared values and goals, mutual respect, and a balance of power. However, do not take my word for it; let's hear from entrepreneurs whose cofounders are also their spouses.

"For us, running a business together and being married seems a natural fit," answers Malgosia Green. She is one of the founders of Savvica, a company that produces the online learning manage-

ment system, Nuvvo. Malgosia elaborates that *"The same things you need to have a successful marriage are required for a successful business partnership – without these key elements, you're up the creek in either endeavor."* She should know, after all, Malgosia not only founded Savvica with John Green, but married him too!

Similarly, David and Stephanie Ciccarelli, cofounders of Voices.com state:

> *"A co-founder needs to be a good communicator, a person with whom you have synergy, and a friend. A healthy business partnership is comparable to a marriage, built on a solid foundation of trust, respect, and understanding. When two complementary business people come together to form a company, guided by the same vision and values, they are at the very heart of their corporate family, and nurture the business as parents would their children."*

Their comments specify the commonalities between the family and corporate union and need not be taken lightly. As manifest in their success, the Ciccarellis know what they are talking about. When it comes to the criteria a life mate and business partner must satisfy. They have recently been rewarded with a nomination for the Young Entrepreneurs award, which showcases young entrepreneurs between the ages of 19 to 35 who have distinguished themselves by their business sense and innovative spirit.

Still not buying it? Let's take a look at the founders of British Columbia born Flickr, Caterina Fake and Stewart Butterfield, who are yet another set of successful married founders. Together they created the on-line photo sharing global sensation, known as Flickr, which was sold to Yahoo last year for millions.

One only needs to look at their monstrous success to confirm their expertise in making both types of partnership work.

The Original Source

Now that we have those in the know agreeing that the parallel between marriage and entrepreneurship is not solely in my head, let's revisit the Rabbi's speech and see what we can learn.

The passage from which he extracted his original text, comes from the Babylonian Talmud - written over 1500 years ago. It reads:

> *Tractate Erovin, page 65b (Rabbi Ilai says) [The nature of] a person is recognized through three things - his Kos (cup, i.e. how he acts after drinking), his Kis (wallet, i.e. business integrity), and his Ka'as (sword, i.e. anger).*

Although I was unable to track down the original Rabbi who delivered the lecture, I did the next best thing. I sat down and enjoyed coffee with Rabbi Rafi Lipner, who runs a non-affiliated drop in centre, dubbed the *HOUSE,* in Toronto. At the *HOUSE,* Jewish education is taught by Rabbi Rafi, who himself was schooled in Talmudic interpretation at the Yeshiva University in New York. Over coffee, he shared his expert opinion with me and explained that:

"The cup, the sword and the wallet, is really a barometer for gauging a person's internal nature in different situations when their inhibitions are lowered and then seeing how those results fit with yours. So yes, I think it does apply to any sort of partner selection, be it domestic or financial".

The following is my interpretation of the Rabbi's explanation of the passage and how I think it might apply to entrepreneurs looking not for a partner in marriage, but a partner in business.

Kos - The Cup

In the original text, Kos or the Cup, refers to how someone behaves after drinking. Rabbinical wisdom says that *when the alcohol goes in, the secrets come out.* Therefore, before you decide to marry someone (or to become their business partner), take them out and get them a little drunk to see what they reveal. Are they Rude? Bullish? Arrogant? Inappropriate? Do their actions under those circumstances mirror yours?

In earlier articles, I often compared the process of raising venture capital to the process of courting for marriage. Hence, it is interesting to note that many investors claim they would not invest in a founder that they could not or would not have a beer with. Although this may just be a figure of speech for some, it does highlight the importance of relationships in commerce and the desire to work with those whose ideals and approaches (especially when under the influence and their guard is down) are similar to yours.

> **Wise Words # 12**
> *Many investors won't fund a founder they couldn't or wouldn't have a beer with.*

One could alternatively or additionally associate drinking with celebratory exuberance and therefore, apply the test to see how his or her business partner handles success. Do they share the joy or focus on the details that went wrong? Do they take all the credit for victory or toast the team? Either way, since success is one of the goals of any venture, it would be insightful to examine their approach and determine whether or not it resonates with yours.

Kis - The Wallet

How someone handles monetary issues is referred to in the passage as *Kis* or the wallet. *Kis* also deals with an individual's business integrity and reveals their priorities in the financial hierarchy. Do they give to charity and their community or hoard it for themselves? Is money a means to an end or an end in itself? Or as the British say "Are you penny wise (no relation), but pound foolish"?

From a commercial perspective I would suggest that *Kis* could also be extended to include equity. How do they see the ownership of the business being split? Do they think their contribution is equal to yours, less, more? What motivates their participation? If partners are not in alignment with respect to monetary issues, there is bound to be a problem down the road, regardless of the business' success or failure. The former is applicable when it comes to dividing profits, while the latter must be addressed when someone has to assume responsibility for the debts.

I would also suggest that monetary issues are just a small part of a business' overall integrity. Business integrity answers the following questions favourably: Do they keep their verbal agreements? Do they share "the wealth" with their employees? Do they take advantage of weaker parties in negotiations? Do they act fairly and with integrity? And do they help others in business without a direct benefit? Guy Kawasaki in his must read book, *The Art of the Start,* dedicated an entire chapter to this concept and called it the Art of being a *Mensch,* (a Jewish word, which is loosely defined as: a decent human being, a good person who always takes the high road.)

Ka'as - The Sword

"Seeing someone happy is important, but seeing how they react when angered is telling," commented the happily married Lipner. He elaborated and acknowledged that *"Everyone gets mad, but what we do when we are furious allows others to see us at our worst."* As noted earlier, this occurs when one's inhibitions are down. It is equally informative to see how your future partner (in marriage or business) handles success and failure. Do they lash out at others or stew internally? Do they accept responsibility or place the blame on everyone but themselves? Do they focus on learning from the situation or ruminate on the cause?

Saying that you will be faced with challenges during your startup's life (or marriage) is similar to saying that you will have to pay taxes every year. This is why it is important to know in the initial stages, how your potential partner deals with hardship. *Ka'as* covers this.

A Few Other Marriage Thoughts:

Further prenuptial metaphors that might be appropriately applied by entrepreneurs considering a business marriage, include:

1. Date First — get to know one another by working on a joint project before agreeing to legally be bound together.

2. Similarities are good — Differences may be better. Being of like mind is important, but opposites often attract. Therefore, make sure you are not just partnering with a clone of yourself. To be truly successful you want your partner to not only have a

different set of skills, but to also be able to challenge your views and strategy. After all, you want to make sure that key decisions are tested and not just agreed to blindly. In essence, you want to find, in both marriage and entrepreneurship, a yin for your yang.

3. Good things are worth working at — in the end, all startups, like all marriages, take work. You want to make sure that both parties are committed to invest the level of work required for the partnership to flourish.

The Bottom Line

It appears that even though the Talmud is more than a millennium old, we can still find relevance in its teachings today. Even though technology and situations may have changed like many ancient texts that capture the wisdom from previous ages, we as people are still pretty much the same. Consequently, whether your marriage is one of domestic bliss or one of financial success, you should be able to minimize your potential for divorce by taking candid stock of your partner, comparing it with yourself and evaluating its congruence. And to do that, all you need is a cup, a sword and a wallet.

Chapter 11

The Power Of A Pictogram

Originally published July 18, 2006

A picture may be worth a thousand words, but a pictogram is worth so much more.

According to Wikipedia (the world's largest free encyclopedia, solely created through end user content, www.Wikipedia.com), pictography is a form of writing whereby ideas are transmitted through drawing. One of the oldest forms of pictography is hieroglyphics. Contemporary versions include what is colloquially referred to in investment circles, as "the back of the napkin diagram". According to Investopedia, the term "back of the napkin diagram" (or for the purpose of this article "BoND") refers to:

> The (pictorial) representation of the basic components of a business model excluding any fine details. The BoND incorporates only the core ideas and success factors of the business. The name comes from the notion that a quick outline of a business can be easily sketched on the back of a napkin to sufficiently demonstrate its fundamental concepts.

In the late 1990s, during the first internet wave, dot.com entrepreneurs would often draw a BoND for the potential investor, as a method of illustrating the ecosystem, value proposition and revenue model of their venture.

Just like the elevator pitch (discussed extensively in an earlier column), the BoND conveys more than what the business does or how it will make money. A strong BoND also illustrates management's passion, focus and most importantly its ability to clearly and concisely communicate the underpinnings of the venture.

But during the early years of the millennium, BoND diagrams became obsolete. This was the case primarily because VCs and Angel investors were moving upstream and focusing on later stages of investment where traction spoke louder than BoND diagrams. Now with the second wave of the internet (dare I say Web 2.0) underway, BoNDs are making a comeback.

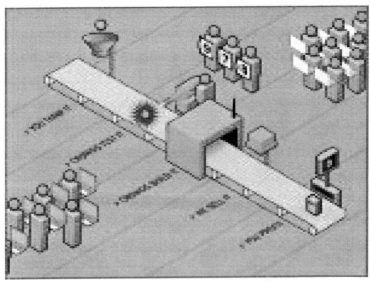

Figure 2: **Sample Bond Diagram for crowdsourcing startup, Cambrian House**

The True Value Of The BoND

Rick Segal, a Partner at J.L. Albright Venture Partners, states that *"Having a great diagram allows the Entrepreneur to have one 'cheat sheet' that lets her tell the story with a compelling visual."* Segal's statement was proven at a SpeedDating for Capital™ event that I hosted last fall, at which 11 Companies met with 10 VCs for 9 minutes each.

Those that had BoNDs in hand were able to employ accuracy and clarity when answering questions posed by the VCs, such as:

> What they were doing?
> Why they were doing it?
> Who benefited from it?
> Who paid for it?

-All questions you need to answer if you are pitching a VC for investment.

Rob Imrie, CEO of DemandCast, was at the SpeedDating for Capital™ event and was one of the entrepreneurs who pitched with a BoND firm in hand. He explains, *"Our diagram helped us to focus the conversation and ensure that we were able to keep the attention of the potential investors. It also showed that we understood the big picture and were focused on end users and the value our technology platform brings to them."* And Imrie should know. His venture later went on to be named "Best Seed Deal in Canada" at the 2006 Canadian Venture Forum. *"Without a pictogram of our solution, not everyone would easily see*

> **Wise Words # 13**
> *Visual diagrams can serve as a powerful platform for conversation.*

all the moving parts and value that our solution provides - at least not as readily."

But BoNDs are not just used to attract investors. A good BoND can also assist with employee recruitment, team alignment, and sales and technology build outs. Segal comments, that *"As the prospective client, employee, or VC engages, both parties can use the drawing as a central reference point. It's a very useful tool that is often overlooked in favour of mountains of text laden painful power point slides."* In fact, BoNDs can be used throughout the business, according to the Grandfather of business visualizations, Dave Gray, Founder and CEO of Xplane (the business visualization company behind the powerful BoNDs you see in Business 2.0 magazine): *"Visual diagrams can serve as a powerful 'platform for conversations.' They help people focus their attention and understand new ideas better and faster. Better understanding leads to better decisions, which leads to better business results,"* said Gray.

Marketing guru, Peter Evans, Partner at Riverdale Partners, a consultancy that specializes in helping its B2B clients take complex technologies to the market, agrees with Gray's statement.

"Technology at the feature level just doesn't sell," says Evans. He elaborates, *"That's why visualizations are so important. They can immediately help you connect with non- technical decision-makers — these are often the people who are major influencers in the purchase decision."*

What makes a Good BoND?

The secret to developing coherent visualizations, according to Evans, lies in the ability to briefly and clearly articulate a number of concepts that provide a richer context for various audiences. Start by thinking about how your solution can be visualized in the following ways:

1. Show the Ecosystem: How does your solution fit together with other technologies and partners across the market landscape from an "interoperability" perspective? Can you draw all these relationships out to show how they work together to provide a seamless solution?

2. Functions and Benefits: Show how your solution works in a detailed way. But do not just focus on function. Take the opportunity to richly describe the benefits that you generate along the way for your end users and customers. Do not forget to show who is paying whom. After all, if exponential value is being delivered you should be able to show how such value can be readily monetized.

3. Before and After: Paint a vivid picture of the points of pain (the business' problems) that your customers experience today. In a separate diagram, consider showing how your solution resolves these issues.

How to build a BoND

In order to map out the steps required to create a powerful BoND, here is the process that Gray recommends:

1. First, be sure you are solving the right problem. The most common reason people have difficulty solving a business or creative problem is because of the way the problem was defined. The best way to define a communication problem is to find the question you want to answer with the communication. Define communications goals as a question that the diagram will answer. For example:

"How does this software work?" "What business result can I expect?" "What's unique and different here?"

2. Don't worry about your drawing skills. If you know the subject, just draw what you know. People don't need pretty pictures; what they care about is your ideas. Stick figures, boxes and lines are good enough to get your point across.

3. Think about your story. Even before we had the written word, a story was the way that humans made sense and meaning out of a complex world. Remember, the BoND's first job is to support a story, and help you have meaningful conversations on a subject you care about. If any part of the picture doesn't support your story, maybe it doesn't belong.

4. Minimize the number of elements. Research shows that people construct mental models in very predictable ways. When asked to diagram a system, the average person uses around six or seven visual elements to support their story. This is true whether they are diagramming something simple, like a toaster, or something complex, like the Houses of British parliament. So keep it simple: If you use much more than six or seven components in your picture, the average person will not be able to follow you, or fully grasp your ideas.

5. Edit ruthlessly, using your goal as a filter. As you create your diagram, use your "goal question" to determine what stays in and what goes. Ask yourself, "Is it helping answer the question at hand?" When in doubt, leave it out.

6. Once you have a visual diagram that you like, ask yourself, "Is it replicable?" The answer is yes if: You can draw it on a whiteboard and tell the story in 10 minutes or less; You can teach someone else to draw the picture and tell the story.

86

7. Once you have something you like, test it on everyone you can — friends, family, your spouse, etc. Keep working on it and adjusting it 'til you feel comfortable with it. Realistically, your story is a living thing and will change somewhat every time you tell it.

8. Revise and update the BoND often - like a good relationship or a good wine, it will only improve over time.

The Process Not Just The Picture

"A pictogram can be an invaluable aid in creating a quick, impactful and clear explanation of a company's service or product, and they often lead to a far greater retention of the details" says Paul Gilligan (www.PaulGilligan.com), one of Canada's most successful commercial illustrators and a local leader in developing BoNDs who worked with Imrie on DemandCast's BoND.

It is interesting to note, that while the end product is obviously the most valuable piece in the process, the process itself can be helpful. According to Gilligan, the process of creating a BoND forces founders to communicate their ideas to people who may not be as well versed in their industry or space. *"I've done quite a few (pictograms) for companies, especially startups, lately. Sometimes entrepreneurs are too close to the forest, to see the trees,"* quips Gilligan. He continues by saying, that *"Working on a back of the napkin diagram forces them to step back and take in the entire landscape and that in and of itself can be tremendously valuable."*

That is something that Tom Sweeney, General Partner of one of Canada's newest early stage funds, Garage Technology Ventures Canada, agrees with wholeheartedly:

"The exercise of generating these powerful sketches is at least three-fold: (1) it forces focus; (2) the product-market concept drives attention onto the value of the innovation; and (3) it allows for the company's story to be carried further, faster and easier by others who may know investors that might be interested in the company's space."

Sweeney's point harkens back to one of the powers of the Elevator Pitch, as it helps mitigate against broken telephone. After all, no matter who you pitch to, they are likely to share your pitch with others and a BoND like an Elevator Pitch raises the probability that the pitch passed along will remain consistent with the original concept.

The Bottom Line

If you are seeking capital today or just looking to nurture your venture organically, you need to be able to describe your venture to anyone and everyone you meet in a way that ensures the message's clarity is preserved. Dedicating time and energy when creating a pictogram or Back of the Napkin Diagram is most likely one of the most profitable things any entrepreneur can do. After all, as previously mentioned, a picture may be worth a thousand words, but a Back of the Napkin Diagram is worth so much more.

Chapter 12

Ready For A First Date With Your VC?

Originally published August 23, 2006

During the last 7 years, I have heard more than 400 pitches annually from entrepreneurs seeking capital from investors. On the set of the CBC's new venture capital reality show, the *Dragons' Den*, I have heard more than 120 pitches in the last 8 days alone. What do all of these pitches have in common, whether in reality or on reality TV? The answer is that they all revolve around a number of key questions that most investors wish to cover in the first encounter a.k.a the "First Date."

The bottom line is that all investors want to make money / a return on their investment and in order to do this, it is imperative that they evaluate your potential to facilitate their goals. This assessment includes the evaluation of answers to two main queries:

1. Is this a deal for me (i.e. does it meet my investment criteria)? And;
2. At what price would this be a deal for me (i.e. can I make enough off of this deal)?

In order to evaluate the opportunity using these key criteria, investors strive to obtain answers to a series of questions. As previously articles have alluded to, investing is much like a courtship. There is a "get to know each other period" (i.e. due diligence), before the commitment. Consistent with this metaphor are several key questions, in no particular order, that you must be prepared to answer on the first date with your potential investor.

If you are looking for capital from angels, venture capitalists or even on a reality TV series, you must not only anticipate these key queries, but you need to formulate your answers in advance, in order to improve your chances for investment.

What Is It That You Do?

> **Wise Words # 14**
> *Formulate answers to key investor questions in advance to improve your chances for investment.*

I know this one seems easy, but you would be surprised at how long it takes some entrepreneurs to communicate their elevator pitch. You only have 60 seconds to relay information concerning the business you are in, the capital you are seeking and why investors should be interested.

In previous columns, the importance of the elevator pitch has been stressed, and as a recap, it is critical that it satisfy these four criteria:

1. Succinct – under a minute or two;
2. Comprehensible – no technologically specific terminology;
3. Undisputable – makes sense; and
4. Greed inducing – it should be apparent that you can make money.

Therefore, be prepared and remember that you only get one chance to make a first impression, so practice ;your elevator pitch with everyone and anyone who will listen. Moreover, ensure your pitch evolves to a universal point where both your toddler nephew and senior great aunt, not only understand what you do, but want to invest.

Why Is What You Do Needed?

This is all about how you will alleviate the "pain." No matter the product or service, there has to be a need for it. This need is often associated with a source of pain. Take the following examples as illustrations of pain in the market and their corresponding solutions:

1. I have too much junk in my basement that others might want, but I cannot sell it to them myself

   = eBay

> **Wise Words # 15**
> *No matter the product, there has to be a need for it.*

2. Hackers keep trying to infect my computer

   = Symantec

3. People want accessible e-mail away from their desks

   = RIM's Blackberry

4. Carrying around a boom box is too cumbersome

   = Sony's Walkman

Investors want to know that there is a need for what you are building. The greater the need, the quicker the sales uptake and the higher the revenue grows, means less cost in convincing customers to buy your solution. Sunil Selby, Managing Director of Trellis Capital, a Toronto based BC Fund, puts it this way:

> *"To get interested in a business opportunity, I look for the entrepreneur to clearly, concisely and well articulately communicate if and how the company's product offering meaning fully increases customer revenues or reduces costs."*

After all, if there is no pain and hence no need for what you are doing ... then why do it?

What Traction Do You Have?

Traction refers to progress, or the concrete milestones that you have reached and surpassed. Investors, for the most part, seek to evaluate and later mitigate three key types of risk, namely:

1. Management Risk: Can these founders deliver?

2. Magic Risk: Can the product be built? And if so, will it be exponentially better?

3. Market Risk: If the founders deliver and the product works, will anyone buy it?

Traction speaks to these issues. Investing in a company that has significant sales indicates that management, to an extent, has built a product that the market is interested in. BDC's Steve Abrams, illustrates the importance of the quality of sales and not just its quantity. "Sales are good, but we also look for the 'Marquee Customer.' Early stage companies may have a few local sales, but its ability to attract a major reference account goes a long way."

Since there is a direct correlation between the risk that investors take and the reward that they seek in return (i.e. The Risk: Return Ratio), a company that has traction will not need to offer as much of a return when compared with a company that does not. To that end, traction not only affects valuation, but also the type of investors you will want to attract. For instance, it would be in the interest of companies without traction to focus on family and friends, while a company with sufficient traction and aspirations to expand, falls more appropriately into the venture capital arena.

Who Else Believes?

An old adage in investment circles expresses that, "You can't be the only one drinking the kool-aid." This comment deals with both third party validation and traction. The former asks, "who else believes that what you are doing is needed and a good idea?" Third party validation is critical; without it, all the investor has is the word and enthusiasm of the entrepreneur, who is trying to sell the idea and by definition is in conflict, since they are the ones seeking the cash.

So what is the best form of third party validation? Simply states, it is sales. Nothing says that your product will sell massive quantities better than the commendable sales to date. If you can

> **Wise Words # 16**
> *You can't be the only one drinking the kool-aid.*

show that customers are begging to buy your prototype, demanding to join your beta test (i.e. trials) or lined up to license it, then you have not only secured third party validation, but you have also achieved traction.

As discussed above, nothing impresses a potential investor more than traction. Trellis Capital's Selby agrees, reminding us that not all "sales traction" is "pure revenue." *"While the best proof of traction is the amount of revenue a company has generated from the sale of its product, the quality of the sales funnel and pipeline, and the entrepreneur's understanding of the customer's purchasing priorities, process and time-line also provides increased comfort that the company's commercialization is moving in the right direction."*

However, if you are too early in the entrepreneurial process to have sales, not all hope is lost. There are other forms of third-party validation. The list is as follows, in descending order of impact:

- Sales
- Large leading Corporate entities in your field have partnered with you
- Joint Ventures with other small players
- White Papers from future customers
- Industry reports from large investment banks and research companies

Yes, I know, Forrester and Garner (well-known industry analysts) are often wrong, but they are more reliable than entrepreneurs seeking cash from investors, at least from an investment perspective. After all, an analyst that is constantly wrong will not be an analyst for very long. Similarly and more to the point, every entrepreneur pitching for cash claims that they have the best product, the best team and the best opportunity - and investors have no choice but to disregard these claims due to the internal conflict of the entrepreneur.

How Much Do You Need?

"How much capital should I ask investors for?" is a question that is often posed to Dan Mothersill and I following our Boot camps on raising capital. The answer, of course is different for every company, but in general the benchmark I give is defined in this way:

> *"Get enough money to make sure you can make it past the next critical milestone, whatever that may be."*

It is necessary to deploy enough capital, so that when you go to the market looking for more, you have successfully moved the company forward to its next critical point. This point is directly linked with the company's key milestones, including but not limited to: finishing a product, filing patents, launching a beta, completing a beta, selling the first product, scaling up sales, and reaching the break even point.

You have to ensure that by the time the money depletes, you have successfully moved the company forward, exponentially added value, and mitigated one of the three risk criteria (management, marketing, magic), so that you can now raise new funds to meet future goals. Investors have little appetite for a company that fails to hit its growth milestones and is now in search of additional funds. Instead, investors often punish the founders of these situations by providing very punitive valuations.

> **Wise Words # 17**
> *Investors have little appetite for a company that fails to hit milestones.*

Consequently, investors not only want to know how much you need, but what the goal of such an investment will be and what goals you have already met.

....*continued next month*

Chapter 13

14 First-Date Questions Investors Will Ask

Originally published September 13, 2006

Last month, investors shared some of the questions they ask entrepreneurs on a "first date" or first meeting with entrepreneurs looking for cash - covering questions, including:

- What is it that you do?

- Why is such needed?

- Who else agrees with you? And

- How much capital do you need?

This month, the so called "First Date" questions turn more specific as investors begin to explore the opportunity more fully.

What are you going to do with my cash?

A tangent of "How much do you need?" which deals with the total capital required to hit the next milestone is often "What are you going to do with it?"

While the former question is macro in nature and focuses on the milestones of development, the latter question is micro, in that it tests an entrepreneur's understanding of their business.

Investors want to know that there is a thought out "spend plan" for their investment. They seek comfort in entrepreneurs that have thought through the deployment of each dollar and to an extent, investors must agree with the entrepreneur's spending blueprint. Like valuation, which will be discussed below, this is not a question of being right or wrong, but one of reasonableness.

Five years after the investors have offered their money, they are not going to care if you bought 5 servers instead of 4, hired 10 sales staff instead of 12, or paid $25/ft for office space instead of $22. After all, it is impractical to predict such outcomes.

However, what investors will want to check is threefold:

- Do I agree with the overall deployment weighting (i.e. % into R/D vs. % into Sales vs. % in infrastructure, etc.)?

- Are the figures well researched and realistic (i.e. has it been priced properly)?

- Is there enough cash to hit the milestones (as discussed above)?

Typically entrepreneurs underestimate the costs, and this concerns investors, not just because it shows a lack of domain knowledge and business acumen, but because it might leave the company short of cash and in turn, short of hitting a key milestone.

It used to be that business plans contained a brief chart regarding use of proceeds. According to Warren Bergen, Executive Director of the Alberta Deal Generator, whose group has looked at hundreds of deals to invest in: *"The three lines would generally split the gross amount of the funding between areas like R&D, working capital and marketing. That certainly does not cut it any more.*

Entrepreneurs that are properly prepared to speak with the finance community will arrive with a detailed finance plan."

How Much Is It Worth (i.e. What's Your Valuation)?

The answer is not an easy one, but at its core, it relies on both intrinsic and extrinsic factors.

Intrinsically, you can judge value based on revenue traction, money invested into the venture to date and intellectual property created to date. So, a company with positive revenue, for instance, $1M in R&D and 5 patents, would be worth more than a pre-revenue company that has only invested sweat equity into the business.

Extrinsic factors can be more complex. These generally refer to items that impact the supply and demand of capital in your region and include, but are not limited to:

> **Wise Words # 18**
> *Your valuation relies on both intrinsic and extrinsic factors.*

- How many other deals is the investor looking at right now?

- What is the quality of those deals?

- How aligned is your opportunity with the investment mandate and methodology?

- What other deals has the investor made recently and how do those deals compare with yours?

- What is the perceived terminal value (i.e. what the VC can sell you for after 5-7 years) of your venture?

As you have no doubt concluded by now, there are a number of indicia which factor into valuation, and a great number of them are highly subjective. This is why VCs often refer to valuation as an art and not a science. *"Many entrepreneurs neglect to examine the current market conditions regarding value. Getting a read on comparative deals of recent histor, will provide some benchmark data to help validate what investors will pay, which matters significantly more than arithmetic models of measure."* says Bergen.

Notwithstanding, valuation is a negotiated item and most investors only ask "what is it worth" or "what per cent do I get for my money," at the initial meeting - not as part of negotiation, but as a sanity check. Investors want to gauge your "reasonableness". After all, if what you are seeking is too far from what they deem reasonable, investors will often simply pass on your pitch, knowing that it will be too hard to reach a middle ground. Worse yet, if what you are seeking is so incongruent with the marketplace, investors may begin to question the prudence of your business judgment. As was previously mentioned, that valuation is not about right or wrong, it is about reasonableness.

Why You?

Once you have proven that there is a market for what you want to sell, investors will often turn their attention away from the product and markets and towards you, the founder.

This question is a chance for you to explain why it is that you are uniquely qualified to build your business. According to David Hornik, General Partner of VC firm August Capital and Professor at Stanford's Graduate School of Business, there are two good answers to this question, either:

1. Here is my background, which makes me uniquely qualified to understand the problem my startup is trying to solve or

2. Here are the circumstances that have led to me getting overwhelmingly excited about the problem my company is trying to solve.

Hornik says that the one answer he hates is "after a lot of research, I decided that there was a big opportunity to make money in X." According to this early stage software investor, *"Money flows from passion and expertise, not from market research"*.

Another reason for the "Why you?" question is risk mitigation. Investors try to evaluate where it is possible to mitigate key risks. Management is of course the largest risk of all. It is possible to change market focus or even upgrade a product, but fixing management is more challenging. Rest assured, there are only a few investors that will offer a term sheet, which does not allow them to change management if need be, but doing so is often a long and painful process.

To preclude management turnover, what do you look for in a managing team?

- **Business Acumen** — the skills needed to manage a high growth venture.

- **Domain Knowledge** — experience in the field the venture is penetrating and a network of contacts in such a field.

- **Operational Experience** — more than just theory, experience executing and a track record of delivering.

In a nutshell, investors want to know that you have the knowledge of, contacts in and a history with the market you are tackling. Do you need all three? No. However, the less you have, the higher the risk the greater the reward you will have to offer investors, which means a corresponding downward slide on the traction chart, as presented above.

What Are Your Goals?

As discussed, investment is often like a marriage. Hence, it is critical to ensure that the goals of both parties are aligned. Investors want to verify that the entrepreneur's goals are consistent with theirs. If not, there is potential for trouble down the road.

Investors typically want a 10x return on their money at the seed stages, where the risk is greatest, and a 5x return on their money when traction is accumulating. If a founder of a pre-revenue start-up is busy offering a 10 per cent return on the money lent to them, it is unlikely that a deal will be reached.

> **Wise Words # 19**
> Investors want to verify that the entrepreneur's goals are consistent with theirs.

This often affects valuation, as the investor needs to make sure that she or he owns enough of the company, so when it hits its terminal value (i.e. the imaginary future price at which a company value is maximized and then crystallized through a liquidity event — when the company is sold), their share is large enough to generate a return on the risk they have taken.

Beware however, that most investors are not interested in dividends or supporting businesses for life. They want to invest, facilitate business growth, sell the business, and finally collect a return on their investment. If your business cannot go public or be sold in five to seven years, it might be hard for investors to do this. Discussing potential exits requires more than simply stating that "we plan to undertake an IPO or M&A transaction after five years." You need to show that potential acquirers are out there and subsequently, fuel the imagination and greed of potential investors by showing them why these large companies will want to buy you. Convey to the investors that you have given some thought to this, even if it still remains in the far future.

How Did You Come Up With This?

This is a chance for the entrepreneurs to shine. It is a chance to tell your story. But you must be careful and understand the true meaning behind this question. The true meaning is to peer inside the motivation of the entrepreneur.

For the most part, investors only want to support those founders that they like and feel that they can work with. If a wonderful deal comes their way, but the founder is too hard to collaborate with or has unrealistic aspirations, investors will often pass. The reason for this is multifold, but generally centers round the fact that a start-up business is hard enough to deal with, independent of founder egos and unreasonable expectations.

Then there is the question of underlying motivation. Steve Abrams, from the BDC venture capital group, explains it like this:

"To me the question: 'Why the founder came up with this idea and solution' is more important than we let on. I know, after years in the investment game, that it is a rough road ahead, even with funding. So I want to know that the founder is passionate about this and in love with what they are doing. I need to know that they are 150 per cent committed to the venture, and will do whatever it will take to make the business succeed."

What Stops Me From Taking It To China?

Or what stops Microsoft from copying it? This question re-volves around barriers to entry. If you were able to build your product for under $100K, what prevents others from doing the same? And if others decide to replicate it, what happens to our investment?

In today's business world, anything can be copied, reverse en-gineered and knocked off. That is why

> **Wise Words # 20**
> Investors tend to risk their money on ventures that are tackling billion dollar sized mar-kets.

patents and other forms of IP are important. But IP is not enough. You have to show that your advantage is greater than just a legal right to sue those who copy you. You must show that it will be easier for a big player (ex. Microsoft), to buy your venture, as opposed to building a competitive

product. In that way you can kill two birds with one stone, show that you have a competitive advantage and map out pos-sible exit strategies.

How Big Is This Market? How Big Can You Get?

Investors know that at best, your venture is likely to only get a small percentage of market shares. To that end, they want to make sure that this small per cent is on a very large market number. August Capital's David Hornik describes markets in the following manner, *"We measure market size in two flavours — really, really big markets and everything else. We are only interested in funding companies that compete in really, really big markets."*

Investors tend to risk their money on ventures that are tackling billion dollar sized markets. If however, you are not tackling such, then you need to show that you will easily be able to acquire a much larger market share. Either way, market share is directly correlated with revenue growth, and revenue growth is directly linked to terminal value - which in turn affects the return on an investment, and that is all most investors want to know.

If however, your business will plateau at a few million dollars in revenue, it may be difficult for investors to support you. Investors often call such businesses "hobby" or "lifestyle" businesses, and while there is nothing wrong with such per se, they are generally not fundable.

Why? Well, say an investor gives you $500,000 for your pre-revenue business and takes back 40 per cent equity. After five years, the investor will want to receive $3-5M in returns. If the business is only doing a million in sales, how will it be sold at $10M to generate $4M in rewards for investors? Terminal values are most often linked to multiples of revenue, and a 10x revenue multiple seems pretty steep for a small business. There are of course exceptions that disprove the rule, for example, pre-revenue start-ups sold for multiples that approach infinity, but these are of course exceptions and should not be relied upon.

> *Wise Words # 21*
> *Scalability means revenues accelerate quicker than costs.*

How Do You Scale?

Scalability means, as your product rolls out, your revenues accelerate quicker than your costs accumulate. Take software for instance - the most scalable type of business. Once you have done the coding, each sale only costs you the price of burning a

CD - even less if you allow for on-line downloads. Whereas in the case of professional services (the least scalable business), your costs are directly linked to your revenue generators (i.e. the people who work there), making it hard to scale.

A business that cannot be scaled will be stagnant in long- term growth, and this is not attractive to investors. Investors want to know how their money, which will go to cover costs, will lead to exponential revenue growth. Generally, they are not interested in spending a dollar to make a dollar; they want to spend a dollar to make $10 in time.

But investors need to know that it is more than just a pipe dream. According to Warren Bergen, *"Most entrepreneurs speak only in terms of their percentage of market share gained over time without any detailed plan of how to accomplish this task."* A few questions about how growth will be achieved provides insight with respect to how well developed their strategy is. If an entrepreneur can slap down a comprehensive implementation plan, I know I'm speaking with a more sophisticated entrepreneur. If they are at all vague over the "how" this is all going to grow, it's a dead issue, and my Angels are out.

> **Wise Words # 22**
> *The chances of getting funding go down dramatically if the founders aren't fully committed.*

What's Your Skin In The Game?

Nothing frustrates investors more, than being asked to invest in a company that the founders themselves have not fully committed to. According to Steve Abrams, from BDC's Montreal office, *"The chances of getting funded go down dramatically if the founders aren't fully committed. If the founders aren't committed 100 per cent, I sometimes want to say to them 'Don't quit your day job.'"*

Most venture capitalists require the entrepreneur to have a significant portion of their personal net worth tied up in the deal. The reason, according to Bergen is, *"If the entrepreneur does not have enough in the deal, Investors become concerned that when times get tough it will be too easy for the individual or team to walk away, leaving the VC to come in and clean up, and that is not something they want to be stuck doing."*

The term "skin in the game," refers to what founders have at risk. The amount of skin in the game is completely subjective and deals with the personal situations of the founders. For some, it might be a mortgage on the house or maxed out credit cards. For others, it might be the refusal of other employment opportunities or years of hard work. Regardless of their situation, investors need to know that when the going gets tough — you will not get going. They need to know that you have a compelling reason to stay the course and ensure that their money is well looked after.

The Bottom Line

If securing an investment is equivalent to getting married, then the initial pitch is equivalent to the first date. And like most first dates, making a good impression is vital. So whether you are pitching on reality TV, or to a VC, make sure you prepare answers to these common questions in order to increase your chances of getting a second date.

Chapter 14

Leverage Your Board

Originally published October 24, 2006

Not only am I currently the Chair of two public companies, but I sit on the Boards of non-profit organizations, as well as the Board of Advisors to a number of other organizations and venture funds. Consequently, I know first hand that strong boards can be an entrepreneur's dream asset or a founding CEO's worst nightmare.

Len Brody, author of several books on Entrepreneurship, put it best:

"Boards are like a flu shot: Nobody likes getting one, it stings at first, then it leaves a long lasting bruise and sucks your energy. But, in the end, it protects you from unforeseen harm and, for all the grief, you are eventually glad you had it done. So much so, you end up getting one every year."

So, how can you ensure that you get the most out of your Board? Easy — Leverage.

> **Wise Words # 23**
>
> *Strong boards can be an entrepreneur's dream asset or a founders worst nightmare.*

Archimedes, the Greek mathematician and physicist (and coincidentally, the coiner of the term "Eureka"), described leverage in 300 BC, as a means for converting a small force into a larger one - often employed to move a heavy obstacle.

The obstacles to an entrepreneur are heavy indeed: under resourced, overworked, under-funded, breaking new ground, lacking product credibility and venture brand. But the same principles can be used by entrepreneurs in small early stage startups to gain traction and move the heavy obstacles in their way (ex. first customers). Just as the lever and fulcrum, through proper deployment, enabled Archimedes to lift several times his capacity, the leveraging of a Board enables an entrepreneur to accomplish much more than his resources seem to dictate.

The Board Defined

By law, incorporated companies must have a Board of Directors.

In the earliest stages of a venture, the Board of Directors is often limited to shareholders who are simultaneously the active founders and active management of the business. These early Boards tend to be informal and highly unstructured. As the company progresses and outside investment is injected into it, the Board of Directors will usually grow to include new external shareholders, who wish to be kept apprised of the company's activities. If the shareholder base evolves to include institutional financiers or if formal investors (ex. Venture Capitalists) become involved, the Board of Directors may likewise evolve into a more structured and formal entity.

The Role Of The Board

The legal requirements for a Board of Directors are set out in the Corporations Act. The Board of Directors is typically responsible for supervising management, reviewing the financials, appointing senior management and most importantly safeguarding the best interests of the shareholders. Collectively, these duties are often referred en masse as "Corporate Governance."

110

However, while these duties may satisfy the Boards' legal requirements, the true role of the Board often runs much deeper.

"The right Board of Directors is an important asset to any organization but especially a start-up," states Vikas Gupta, CEO of Transgaming Technologies. *"Boards play many different roles, but for young companies, a board can serve as an extension to the management team and can round out the requisite experience and expertise that is necessary to launch a start-up to success,"* Gupta comments. *"The board should provide a management team with objective feedback on a company's strategy, should challenge the management team to ensure the team has the appropriate levels of conviction and defensibility for their ideas and, perhaps, most importantly, provide support and motivation towards the successful execution of the approved business plan."*

Hence, in addition to providing formal legal governance, a Board often assumes some or all of the following roles:

- Accountability: Just as employees report to the CEO, the CEO in turn should report to the shareholder base. But to facilitate such efficiently, a Board is elected by shareholders to represent their interests. Thus, the CEO reports to the Board. In doing so, s/he becomes accountable.

- Sounding Board: Management needs an echo chamber to bounce ideas off of and to ensure that decisions are made in due course with the use of a deliberative process.

- Mentoring the CEO: Being a CEO can be lonely and frustrating. Therefore a resolute CEO will often leverage the Board as mentors; leaning on their experience to enhance his or her own.

- Extending the Network: Strong board members will bring access to customers, finance and sales channels. And finally

- Filling in the Holes: Startups are often under-resourced Until full-time staff is retained for all positions, Board members can often assist management in specific areas of operations (ex. interviewing key staff, hammering out financing, arranging bank facilities, etc.).

Board Composition

The size of the Board of Directors is established by constituting documents of the company, but is always subject to change. So, in the end, the size of your Board is a matter of choice. For pre-revenue companies, I usually recommend a three-person Board, but for later stage companies, a five-person board is often more suitable. If the Board is too large, it may become unwieldy, making it difficult to co-ordinate schedules for meetings which, early on, should be held monthly. In contrast, if the Board is too small, you will fall short on the opportunity to maximize the leverage that a Board can generate. Once the Board's overall size has been determined, you should balance its composition by recruiting from management, the shareholder base, and most importantly, from the industry.

> **Wise Words # 24**
> *If the Board is too small, you lose the opportunity to maximize their leverage.*

On a five person Board of Directors, post outside investment, the following structure is recommended:

- The CEO;

- Another key member of Management, i.e. possibly the CTO or the VP of Sales;

- A representative of the founding shareholders or the early investors;

- A representative of shareholders from the last round of investment; and

- An independent Chairperson.

Since they themselves have no vested interest, it is key to have an independent Chair who will often act as a balance between competing interests. With regard to filling the independent seat(s) on the Board of Directors, founders should use these opportunities to fill holes in the venture's Talent Triangle.

In an earlier article, I discussed the theory of the Talent Triangle. It outlined the three equal components of a well-rounded management team as being: Business Acumen, Domain Knowledge and Operational Experience. Commonly, startups cannot afford to recruit top talent to fill these corners. In such cases, the composition of the Board can be used to compensate. A few examples include the following:

> **Wise Words # 25**
> *A well rounded management team is made up of equal parts: Business Acumen, Domain Knowledge and Operational Experience.*

1. If management has never taken a startup to greatness, they might be weak in the area of Business Acumen (i.e. How to run the business). In this scenario, it might be best to recruit a mentor who has experience for the Board. This mentor might

come in the form of a serial entrepreneur, an Angel Investor, or a professional service provider.

2. If management lacks in-depth client knowledge or needs a better customer network, then its Domain Expertise is inadequate. To compensate leverage the Board, by nominating either future clients, those who sell to your future clients or leading experts in the field, i.e. anyone who is exceptionally knowledgeable about your industry or has an incessant domain rolodex.

3. If management's operations experience is low, then recruit to the Board those who have built and distributed similar products and leverage their experience. In high tech start-ups, operational experience can be obtained by recruiting experts from companies in different domains with similar product lines, i.e. selling shoes on-line is different than selling books, but from an operational perspective they are more similar than different.

One final note on independents and the Board comes from a reformed venture capitalist and current manager at Calgary Technologies Inc., Kerri Knull, who shares with us another key benefit of having independents on the Board:

"An uneven balance of VC's (investors) and founders on your board can often set the stage for tension-filled meetings where the business of the company's growth is secondary. To avoid such a situation, work closely with your investors to select independent board members that balance the blend of personalities on your board along with relevant domain experience and a history of business success."

Investors And The Board

As mentioned above, investors often want to take a seat o the Board, to monitor the activities and growth of the company as well as their investment In the case of venture capital investors, this is almost always the case. But what role does the Board play, pre-investment?

I asked Robin Axon, Vice-President of one of the oldest VC funds in Canada, Ventures West, the role that Boards play pre and post investment. *"We wouldn't invest in a company because of the Board makeup alone, but an impressive Board made up of relevant industry experts is great validation for a company, and provides an easy starting point for a VC's due diligence. You are definitely judged by the company you keep. And your Board is the greatest example of that."*

Therefore, if raising capital is a future goal, you might want to recruit Board members that are well respected by potential funding sources. Moreover, if you are raising funds, you might want to add members to your Board, who have reputable VC contacts, as was discussed in a previous column on the importance of relationships in the capital raising process. After all Venture Capital is a business that, like so many others, is heavily based on relationships.

The Advisory Board

For the past half decade, the liability associated with being a director - even an independent one for a private company - has continued to grow. This has led to a decrease in the availability of independent directors and even for those businesses with full D&O, i.e. Directors' and Officers', liability insurance, the pool continues to shrink. The easiest way to get past this is to have potential Directors join an Advisory Board.

While a Board of Directors is required by corporate law, a Board of Advisors (i.e. an Advisory Board) is a loosely established committee formed by management to undertake and enhance the formal Board of Directors and management as a whole. Corporate law spells out a list of minimum tasks that a Board of Directors must undertake. For the Board of Advisors however, no such list exists. (Note: For the remainder of this article, the term "Board(s)," shall be used to describe both the Board of Directors and Advisors).

You should recruit your Advisory Board based once again on the Talent Triangle model. Fill perceived or actual holes in management expertise and experience with seasoned veterans.

Compensation and Recruitment:

Irrespective of which Board they sit on, all independent members, i.e. those not receiving compensation as management, should be offered a reward to offset the risk they take and the opportunity cost of dedicating their time to the venture. Once upon a time, options (i.e. stock options from the Employee Stock Option Plan) might have been enough, but today, my experience shows this is rarely still the case. If you expect Board members to dedicate several hours a month to increasing shareholder value, then you need to reward them accordingly.

Founders should be prepared to set aside real funds in return for a Board member's time and energy. This can be paid on a per meeting basis or quarterly and should be in addition to stock options in the company. Fees may vary from $500 a meeting to $20,000 a year, (although the latter would be rare for a

116

startup and the result of a Board member dedicating much more than just a few hours a month).

Examining the opportunity cost serves as the easiest way to determine the appropriate level of compensation for a Board member. If you expect an active Board member to dedicate half a day per month to formal meetings and another half for supporting management informally, then you need to examine the opportunity cost of that Board Member. For instance, if that person is a professional service provider, with a per diem rate of $1,000/day, and you want them to meet at least half a day a month, then you should offer them a total compensation package, including options and cash, of at least $3000 a quarter ($3000 in forgone fees, plus a multiple to offset the liability being incurred). The divide between how much of the compensation should be cash and how much should be equity is up to you, but I recommend that the cash be at least equal to the opportunity cost, which allows the equity to offset the risk. Members of the Advisory Board typically get paid less than members of the Board of Directors because of the variance in liability (see below) associated with their role.

Board Alignment

Regardless if they are joining the Advisory Board or the Board of Directors, founders need to ensure alignment with management before nominating a person to the Board. Make sure all parties agree to not only on where the company is going, but on the role they will play.

Some candidates for Board positions see their role as purely fiduciary in nature, and believe that the Board should be strategic and not tactical. As a result, they refrain from getting involved in the day to day operations of the business. Others however, believe that management is simply overtaxed and feel that an effective Board is one that is more active. When recruiting, it is imperative that management discuss these perspectives openly and in depth. You need to ensure that you are "getting what you pay for", and that members of the Board are willing to put in the time and energy management is seeking. If not, you will not be able to fully leverage your board and will only end up with unused potential.

The Dark Side Of Boards

No discussion of Boards would be complete without drawing attention to the down side or dark side of having one. To some, Boards are the ultimate double edged sword.

Some entrepreneurs are not prepared to fetter their authority, while others resent having to report to someone else. An additional group fears that the formalities and costs associated with proper board governance will out-weigh the benefits associated with such. Others fear for their job, as one of the prima facie duties of a Board is the hiring, supervision and firing of the CEO. For some founders, this heavily influences their decision to expand a Board, as they feel it will expose them to intense scrutiny and job insecurity. This is another reason why, investors refer to the Boards of pre-funded companies. If such companies lack a formally active Board, the VC might grow concerned over the entrepreneur's willingness to accept outside guidance, be accountable to others, to undergo scrutiny, and most of all, to do what is right for all of the shareholders and not just the founders.

118

Likewise, there is a downside to being on a Board. As mentioned above, over the last decade the liabilities associated with being on Boards have grown considerably, as has the duty of care expected by each member of the Board. Even with D&O insurance, which can cost upwards of $20,000, even for a small private company, Directors are still exposed to more risk than can be discussed in this article. It is sufficient to say, that agreeing to join a Board is a decision that should riot be taken lightly. Wikipedia, has a great review of the duties and liabilities that Board members should be willing to accept, before formally signing on. And while that article is a good starting point, each potential Board member should seek independent legal advice before accepting their role on the Board.

The Bottom Line

As the Chair of the Boards of several progressive companies, I prefer active Board members, i.e. those who are willing to dedicate a minimum of 100 hours per year to supporting the company. This time will be deployed not just at meetings, but when mentoring the CEO, opening doors to the network and helping to shape the growth strategy of the venture.

> **Wise Words # 26**
> *When recruiting a Board, seek those with the skills, networks and experiences that management doesn't have.*

Despite how much time you want Board members to invest, when recruiting members to your Board(s), seek those with the skill sets, networks and experiences that management does not have. By doing so, you will be able to leverage the talent triangle into a fulcrum that will move obstacles with much less applied force and perhaps one day, like Archimedes, you can shout "Eureka!" in celebration of your success.

Chapter 15

Business Jiu-Jitsu

Originally published November 28, 2006

Business is War. At least that is what a number of authors would have you believe when they apply macro-martial theory to modern business. The best-known case for this is Sun Tzu's, *The Art of War*, in which the legendary Chinese General, Sun Tzu, provides a treatise that has often been sited as fundamental for modern business, namely, the seminal treatise on military strategy.

However, this is the macro view, so what about the micro? If Sun Tzu can teach CEOs how to run global multinationals, who can entrepreneurs turn to to learn the micro-martial strategies required for the victory of their business? In my view, there is but one place to start - The Gracie Family. This family has arguably brought the most powerful martial art, Jiu-Jitsu, from its traditional origins in feudal Japan into the modern age, and in doing so provided entrepreneurs with a treatise of their own.

There are three core reasons for the selection of Jiu-Jitsu as a starting point for an entrepreneurial treatise:

1) The historical art is seen as the foundation of many modern styles of martial arts. This style became formally modernized in the early 20th Century when Mitsuyo Maeda, a master of Japanese Jiu-Jitsu, immigrated to Brazil and taught his system to

Carlos Gracie, who then passed it on to his younger brother, Helio. Thereafter, the Gracie family evolved the art into the modern and established form of Brazilian Jiu-Jitsu (Brazilian Jiu-Jitsu, is the pre-eminent form of unarmed combat, where one takes on all opponents, irrespective of their size or preferred style of fighting). Since that time, the Gracies have seldom been beaten in unarmed, one-on-one, no rules competition.

2) In 1993, an open tournament was held where practitioners of all styles of martial arts competed in one-on-one, no rules combat. It was here that Royce Gracie, master of Gracie Jiu-Jitsu (i.e. Brazilian Jiu-.litsu) reigned supreme. He went on to become a living legend in mixed martial arts, winning the next 3 of 4 Ultimate Fighting Championship (UFC) tournaments, which proved that Gracie Jiu-Jitsu was indeed the most well rounded form of hand to hand combat in the modern world.

3) The parallels between serial entrepreneurs and Jiu-Jitsu experts are extensive, but the most fundamental one is that both remove size from the equation. Similarly, in both Jiu-Jitsu and entrepreneurship, strategy trumps the use of force.

Brazilian Jiu-Jitsu black belt, Professor Rener Gracie, of the Gracie Academy (www.graciceacademy.com) whose grandfather, Helio Gracie, is accredited with helping create the art of Brazilian Jiu-Jitsu. Helio's Uncle, Royce Gracie, is arguably the most recognized professional martial artist in the world after winning UFC 1, UFC 2, UFC 4; and whose style of fighting has proved to be the most all round dominant form of martial arts on the planet. We discussed the fundamental principles of Gracie Jiu-Jitsu and how entrepreneurs might apply such to their everyday quest for victory in the business world.

122

The Guiding Principles Of Gracie Jiu-Jitsu

1. If You Have The Leverage You Do Not Need The Strength

"The most important thing is not how much strength you have but how efficiently you use your strength." says Rener, currently a lead instructor at the Gracie Jiu-Jitsu Academy in Torrance, CA. Before applying this to entrepreneurship, one needs to quickly re-examine the principle of leverage. Referring to my previous column, Leverage your Board, we know that Archimedes defined leverage as the manner in which you can use a key point to allow you to move a disproportionately larger object with less force.

The same is true in small business. First, you must find the key point on which all else rests. In commerce, this is often defined as the KPI, or key performance indicator, the one thing on which the growth of your venture rests. It may be the cost of goods sold, or the cost of customer acquisition, or even patentable intellectual properly, but once you find it you

> **Wise Words # 27**
> *If you train yourself to be comfortable in problematic situations you are never caught off guard.*

need to drive your value through it and continue to leverage it until victory is assured.

2. Prepare For All Worst-Case Scenarios

According to the Gracie family, if you train yourself to be comfortable in problematic situations you are never caught off guard. *"If you prepare for the worst, nothing can surprise you"*, says the California based black belt. The same is true in entrepreneurship, in my experience. You need to be aware of the risks, plan for them, mitigate them to the best of your abilities, but don't fear them.

Addressing risk is most often required when entrepreneurs pitch for capital. Investors grow gravely concerned when an entrepreneur blindly discounts the risks associated with the opportunity. Instead, founders who prepare contingency plans for worst case scenarios, even if there is only a remote possibility of such occurring, comfort investors. Examples of prepared scenarios might include losing a key customer, the denial of a patent or slow sales traction.

3. Position Before Submission

According to Gracie,, before you can focus on victory, which might result from your opponent's submission or a decisive knockout, you must set yourself up for it. He elaborates, *"You need to focus on achieving a good position and the submissions will come."* How does this apply to startups and other forms of high growth companies? Well, the lesson here is fairly straightforward: before concentrating on victory, set yourself up for success and work on achieving a strong market position.

> **Wise Words # 28**
> *Before you can focus on victory, you need to set yourself up for it.*

For instance, if you believe that your KPI is customer satisfaction, then focus all of your energy toward achieving the highest possible degree of customer satisfaction. This in turn, will serve as a precursor for high customer traction and high sales revenue and will eventually lead to victory. Hence, you must first locate the key leverage point of your venture and use it to excel, relative to your competitors.

4. *If You Do Not Lose You Will Eventually Win:*

This was the most challenging principle for me to comprehend, and so I asked Gracie to explain it further. He elaborated, *"If you have good technique and you can avoid defeat long enough, the only possibility left is victory."*

Applying this to entrepreneurial business is tricky, but can be done. If you accept that just as in a fight, business is a war made up of a series of skirmishes, you can see that if you survive through these, you will eventually win the war. As a case in point, let us examine YouTube. The skirmishes in the case of YouTube might include litigation letters from content providers such as Fox and Universal, attacks on market share from video sharing rivals like Google and MSN, and the need to police content. While YouTube might not have won all of these confrontations, they certainly did not lose them, and in the end, they achieved victory, as Google tapped out and submitted by buying them for more than $1.5 billion dollars.

5. *Timing Is Everything*

"The right move at the WRONG time is worthless," comments the third generation warrior, *"the right move at the right time is priceless."* Attendant with setting yourself up for victory, you must be patient and wait for the right moment to strike.

One need look no further than the example of Friendster vs. MySpace to illustrate the importance of timing. While both have at their core, the same fundamental business model and value add to end-users, the former was created in 2002, while the latter emerged in 2003. Friendster is now viewed as having gone before the market was ready for it, compared with MySpace that entered the market at the right time. Google offered to buy the former for $30M, while the latter sold for more than $0.5 billion just 24 months after launching. Why did this happen? It was not due to better technology, marketing or focus, but simply timing. MySpace hit the market just as the couch potato tweens were becoming mouse potato teens, while Friendster went for the knockout and gassed before the second round was complete.

The Canadian Perspective

I was so impressed with Rener Gracie and his insights on the lessons that Jiu-Jitsu can teach entrepreneurs, that I looked up Mark Bocek, one of Canada's first black belts in Jiu-Jitsu and a former student of the Gracie's, to delve deeper into "Business Jiu-Jitsu".

The five time Canadian Champion agrees with Gracie's insights:

> **Wise Words # 29**
> Take the fight to the spot your opponent doesn't want to go.

"*Jiu-Jitsu is one of the world's most powerful martial arts, mostly because it is skill, not size that leads to victory.*"

In addition to the five principles laid out by the Californian Gracie, Bocek suggests entrepreneurs leverage the following insights, which he has learned in his storied career:

1. Take Your Opponent Out Of His Or Her Comfort Zone

"In fighting, like business, you have to choose where you want to focus your energies. I always suggest that you take the fight to the spot your opponent doesn't want to go." This is particularly useful for entrepreneurs to remember when they go to the market with limited resources. Choose a key area, such as price, quality or customer service, where your competitors are weak and channel your limited resources there. By doing so, you will be strong where they are weak, and have a better chance of attaining victory, or as Mark put it, "Dictate where the fight takes place (on the ground, on your feet, in the clinch) and you are able to gain the advantage."

2. Never Stop Learning. The Day You Stop Learning Is The Day You Die

Gracie's Grandfather, the legendary Helio Gracie, at the age of ninety-three, is rumored to still be practicing the art he helped found. Mark asserts: "The moment you sit back, you're done. You have to always be open to learning new things, to making changes in your style and approach, and most of all, you have to be willing to listen to others."

> **Wise Words # 30**
> *You have to be always open to learning new things. You have to be willing to listen to others.*

Therefore, just as in business, Jiu-Jitsu requires flexibility and adaptability.

3. Study Your Opponents

Bocek recommends learning as much as you can about your enemy, before engaging in combat with them. He states, "Knowledge is power. Knowing your enemy allows for preparation. Preparation leads to victory." *Scientia potential est*, the Latin maxim, was coined by Sir Francis Bacon. The phrase, which roughly translates to "knowledge is power," implies that knowledge augments one's abilities and potential in life. I concur with both Bacon and Bocek and find that this maxim is applicable to Entrepreneurship.

The Bottom Line

Just as Sun Tzu taught us that macro military theory has a place in the corporate world, the Gracie Family teaches us that entrepreneurs can learn a lot from the principles of modern Brazilian Jiu-Jitsu. However, if you want to earn your black belt, in either then you must train hard by dedicating yourself to practicing the fundamentals everyday, so that when the opportunity presents itself, you are prepared to seize victory.

Chapter 16

2006: The Year Of The Mob

Originally published January 3, 2007

2006 saw the rebirth of the net's coolness and saw startups once again become the "in" place to work. The sales of YouTube (for more than $1.5B) and MySpace (for more than $500M), showed there was still money to be made by backing startups.

This year also saw a number of new business paradigms come to the fore. I've sifted through many of them, and here are the five that I think every entrepreneur should not only make themselves familiar with, but also consider adopting to fuel their growth, in 2007.

1. The Long Tail
2. The Wisdom of Crowds
3. The Tipping Point
4. Community is King
5. The World is Flat

What's interesting about all these theories is that not since Mary Shelly's novel about Frankenstein have Mobs been so empowered. It also seems that 2006, was the YEAR OF THE MOB.

The Long Tail

Based on Chris Anderson's book of the same name, the Long Tail is a statistical phenomenon which states that the sum of the sales for low demand items, when taken collectively, can equal or exceed the market share of the few blockbuster items that are in high demand if the distribution channel is large enough.

The Long Trail phenomenon is especially relevant in e-commerce. Think about amazon.com. A regular book store, say Coles, has limited shelf space, and thus can only stock those items that are in heavy demand by the majority (i.e. the best-sellers). But Amazon can stock an infinite number of books, since it has no limit of shelf space. Anderson's Long Tail theory says that the sum of all the low demand books sold on Amazon in a day will be larger than sales of the bestsellers. Funny enough, according to the staff at Amazon, he was correct.

How this affects your business: The Long Tail allows experts in smaller domains to reap a benefit that used to be reserved for those who served the masses. Ex. The Long Tail, is on one the reasons that Blogs have taken off. There may not be enough viewers demanding a TV show on making Star Trek costumes, but there are enough readers to warrant a blog on it.

The Wisdom Of Crowds

Although based on a 2004 book by James Surowiecki, 2006 saw this contrarian concept take centre stage. The Wisdom of Crowds theory says that a large group of average people is smarter than an expert. In his book, Surowiecki gives extensive examples of when and how this theory could be best used, but a local example can be seen with the Canadian web 2.0 company, Simply Bullish. Simply Bullish polls a group of regular people on whether or not they feel certain publicly traded stocks will increase or decrease in price. With a large enough sample size, the results of Simply Bullish should, according to Surowiecki's theory, be able to predict market trends more accurately then any Bay street analyst. Simply Bullish is still in beta, but I look forward to seeing the results once they reach the tipping point.

How this affects your business: The Wisdom of Crowds is taken to the next level through the theory of crowd sourcing. Coined by Wired writer Jeff Howe, crowd sourcing occurs when disparate groups of amateurs contribute to the creation of a product. Cambrian House, another leading Canadian Web 2.0 company, applies a crowd-sourcing model to identify and develop profitable software ideas. Using a simple voting model, they attempt to find sticky software ideas that can be developed using a combination of internal and crowd-sourced skills and effort. By doing so, they mitigate the risk of producing products that no one but the original designer wants to use, let alone buy.

The Tipping Point

Like the Wisdom of Crowds and Crowd Sourcing theories, the Tipping Point theory deals with the effects of bringing large communities together. Malcom Gladwell, in his bestselling book of the same name, says that adoption exponentially increase after some key number of users is reached, even if better products come to market.

We can see this with Apple's iPod, which is arguably not the best technical MP3 player in the market, and yet once it reached a certain market adoption point, it became unstoppable.

How this affects your business: In venture capital, investors are always looking for scalable businesses, i.e. those businesses in which revenue grows exponentially faster than costs (ex. Software). For most start-ups, customer acquisition is the most difficult task, and Gladwell shows how positive epidemics can be created on the basis of viral marketing. Don't believe me? Just ask YouTube, Hotmail or Napster.

Community Is King

2006 may go down as the year that Blogs, the online postings of individuals and groups around a topic (think daily column in the newspaper), reached their Tipping Point. As of October 2006, Technorati was tracking more than 57,000,000 blogs collecting billions of visitors weekly. The blogosphere is now doubling more than once a year in size. Yet of most visited sites on the internet, only 12 of the top 100 are Blogs. The reason for this apparent contradiction - the majority of Blogs make up the Long End of the Tail. Notwithstanding, Blogs have proven a key business tool, especially for those who wish to crowd source. Another example of the power of Community is My Space, the online voice of teenagers. As of today, MySpace has over 100,000,000 registered users, and is now generating millions of dollars in ad revenue.

So what's so important about Community? Well besides being able to crowd source ideas and receive ongoing customer feedback in real time, a powerful community can actually generate product. This is called User Generated Content or UGC.

UGC is thus another of the hallmarks of Community. Imagine how long it would take for the founders of YouTube to create even 1 per cent of the videos they host, let alone the millions that are uploaded weekly. By allowing end users to self generate content, the founders of YouTube have effectively outsourced content creation and did so in a manner that not only created viral marketing (i.e. "come see the video I just posted")," but also created the key asset being monetized for practically nothing.

How this affects your business: Previously, start-ups had to limit their customer interaction to your focus groups. Now, with blogging and other community based tools, small businesses can gather customer feedback in real time, allowing them to continually improve their products and increase the probability of market traction.

The World Is Flat

The World Is Flat is the best-selling book by Thomas L. Friedman in which the Pulitzer Prize winning journalist discusses the leveling of the global playing field in business. Where once outsourcing to India and China were the domain of large multinationals, today, even the smallest of businesses can benefit from employing the global mob. Friedman discusses the ever growing connectivity of the world (Blogs, anyone?) where you can send voice, movies and text instantaneously to anyone online.

How this affects your business: Using tools from Skype, Writely and DabbleDB, management teams no longer have to be geographically aligned to run their business. Take recently funded b5 Media, whose founders live in Australia, Canada and New Zealand. Through the magic of web 2.0 internet tools, they are able to effectively run and grow their business globally.

The Bottom Line

In 1818, Mary Shelly showed the dangers of mobs, which, once incited, can wreak havoc. Anderson, Surowiecki, Howe, Gladwell and Friedman conversely show that mobs can be a force of good for those entrepreneurs that know how to leverage them. It is not, after all, the size of the mob, but how you use it that matters in the end.

Chapter 17

Do You Need A Business Plan?

Originally published January 24, 2007

Hundreds of years ago, Magellan, Cabot and Drake explored the world. Their successors, Gates, Page, and Cubin have become the explorers of our new world. Like their metaphorical forefathers, these modern day explorers choose a destination, set a waypoint and set off, constantly retooling and updating their map as they go.

Creating a business plan is a critical step in any new business venture. Would you trek across the country, from Montreal to Victoria, without a map? Would you build a house without a blueprint? Would you bake a cake without a recipe? While some might answer yes to all three of these questions, I would be reluctant to be their travel partner, live in their house or eat their cake.

> **Wise Words # 31**
>
> *Creating a business plan is a critical step in any venture.*

I receive questions from entrepreneurs daily and the best ones are answered on my blog (www.SeanWise.com). Some questions however, are of such importance that they need to be addressed in a larger forum. "Do I need a business plan?" represents one such question. The short answer is yes, unequivocally yes! You need a business plan for your venture, whether it is big or small, a startup or global player, raising money or bootstrapping. You need a plan.

A business plan is a comprehensive statement that includes the objectives of your business and how you intend to achieve them. Unless you are working alone (even then, I think you need a plan), have no need for outside capital, or have not prioritized growth and expansion, you need to write a business plan.

The Top 5 Reasons Why You Need A Business Plan

1. Creates a common starting point:

By its very nature, a Business Plan is a concise statement indicating the current stage of your business. If done correctly, it will contain all the information outside parties such as investors, future employees and bankers, will need to make a decision with regard to your venture. The Business Plan allows your reader to quickly review the key areas, such as management, technology, customers, industry metrics and the financial model. By using a standardized format, readers are able to easily identify your venture's key metrics, models and performance indicators. Without a plan, stakeholders have to rely on the oral representations of management or worse yet, have to review hundreds of documents themselves, before gaining confidence that management is "up to speed."

> **Wise Words # 32**
> *A well written business plan gives stakeholders a common place to start a dialogue.*

According to Benoit Hogue from Propulsion Ventures, a business plan is not so much the document itself, but all of the material and thought that goes into creating the document: *"Founders*

136

should see the business plan as a collection of blocks (i.e. a budget, a product Roadmap and white paper, marketing plan, etc). These blocks when put together really synthesize the entrepreneurs' overall thoughts on the venture."

Not only does it provide a one stop shop for the vital information stakeholders require, but a well written business plan gives stakeholders a common place to start a dialogue, which is extremely important if you are looking for external parties to buy into your venture.

2. Sets the goals & shares your vision:

How do you know where you are going or even when you have arrived, if you do not set goals? Going back to our earlier example of trekking across the country, from Montreal to Victoria without a map, the business plan not only informs your route, but also specifies the destination or "waypoint." Without your final waypoint, you cannot possibly plot your journey. In fact, until you set such, you should not even attempt your endeavour. The same is true for business. If you do not have goals, how will you plot your course? Stephen Covey, who sold more than 15 million copies of his book, *The Seven Habits of Highly Effective People*, said it best when he named goal setting as (i.e. Begin with the End in Mind). The second required habit in his seminal guide to success. He knew that the true role of management is to do just that, manage the business. This necessitates setting goals and tracking the venture's progress toward meeting those goals.

Goal setting is also necessary for the ongoing alignment of teams. Whether that team is made up of other founders or includes outside investors and stakeholders, you need to ensure the team in its entirety is on the same page. This "page" must come from the Business Plan.

Finally, in addition to alignment, goal setting helps you manage your progress and gauge your success. It allows you and the other stakeholders to establish accountability, monitor your progress and if required, adjust your strategy.

3. Sets the path & identifies required resources:

Every business, no matter how small, needs a working plan for the future, detailing where you are now (i.e. the starting way-point), where you want to be (i.e. the final waypoint), how you are going to go from the former to the latter, how long it will take and what resources you need to make it happen.

Business plans assist in identifying the lacking components such as cash, personnel or distribution agreements and when such is required to be in place. Knowing what is needed and when such is needed helps to ensure that timelines are maintained and pursued. Therefore, by writing a business plan, you can swiftly identify the key areas that require more attention. This in turn assists in prioritizing tasks, which is something that entrepreneurs must continually address.

> **Wise Words # 33**
> *A business plan assists in identifying the resources you are lacking.*

A business plan is a blueprint of the steps you will need to take in order to build your business and outlines the resources that are necessary to complete the project.

4. Forces analysis:

Not only does writing the business plan force you to crystallize your strategy and concisely share your vision, but it also forces you to analyze your position, research key strategies and prepare responses to investors' questions.

The process of writing the plan forces management to take a step back, to scrutinize, set assumptions and determine the appropriate course of action. Although I have participated in various forms of strategic planning, I have yet to find one as efficient or effective, as writing a business plan.

Those who refuse to write a plan often find themselves answering key questions in front of investors during a pitch, rather than in the comfort of their own office, when they have the time and bandwidth to give such their due.

5. Creates confidence:

A good plan is one that addresses key questions and lays out a reasonable strategy while concisely conveying management's passion and vision. These types of plans instill confidence in potential investors and other external stakeholders. Specifically stated, VCs and Angel investors not only expect management to do this, but to be able to do it well. In

> **Wise Words # 34**
> *A good plan concisely conveys managements passion and vision.*

this way, a business plan reflects that founders understand what it takes to succeed and are able to convey their vision to achieve success.

Reasons Not To Write A Plan And Why They Are Incorrect

Irrespective of the aforementioned, entrepreneurs who are over-burdened with priorities or are under resourced continue to put forth reasons why they cannot or do not want to write a business plan. Here are a few of my favorites and why they are invalid.

"But I heard investors don't read plans, so what is the point?"

While it is true that some investors might not spend as much time reading full plans as you would like them to, all investors do read the executive summary, which is of course based on the financial and entire business plan. According to Susan Wu, from the Menlo Park office of Charles Rivers Ventures: *"VCs absolutely pay attention to the executive summary. The executive summary is your calling card and it determines whether or not you get to the critical next step - the face-to-face meeting. You should approach the executive summary the same way you would an elevator pitch. Make it: brief, pithy, and tantalizing. Writing a full business plan helps you conceptualize all of the nuances of your business and this understanding is crucial in helping you succinctly articulate your startup's unfair advantage."*

Similarly, most investors will conduct initial due diligence, by discussing with entrepreneurs issues that are covered in the plan. Hence, entrepreneurs need to write a plan, if for no other reason than to prepare for such questions.

"But I'm too busy running my business to write about my business."

Are you too busy driving to fill up the car with gas?

"Can't I just hire a consultant to write my plan?"

It is absolutely fine; in fact I recommend it, to involve others in reviewing your plan. In my opinion however, it is absolutely unacceptable to outsource this task. After all, who else knows your business better than you?

The founders must write their business plans. There are many reasons for this, including, but not limited to:

1. The plan is less important than the process that goes into forming the plan, as stated above. This process, which can take up to hundreds of hours, forces management to consider all factors. If a consultant, here today gone tomorrow, undertakes this process, then all the information and analysis undertaken during the writing of the plan, leaves once the plan is finalized, which is simply unacceptable.

2. As previously relayed, management's most important function is managing and you certainly do not outsource your main function. What message would it communicate if someone else set your strategy?

3. The founders will not only have to speak on behalf of the plan, but live with its consequences. Do you really want someone uncommitted to the project setting the goals, strategies and tactics for the business that you will ultimately dedicate all your waking hours to?

> **Wise Words # 35**
> *View your business plan not as a biblical guide but as a snapshot of strategic belief.*

4. You are supposed to be the expert in your field.

"Business is dynamic. Business plans are static. Isn't your business plan out of date the moment it comes out of the printer?"

Although this might be true, you need to see business planning, as an ongoing process. I ask each of our portfolio company CEOs to revisit their Business Plan at least once a year. This allows for a period of reflection on what worked and what did not, and for adjustments and course corrections to be made en route.

Just as a business evolves, so must a venture's Business Plan. You must therefore, view your Business Plan not as a biblical guide, but as a snapshot of strategic belief that must be revisited and revised on a regular basis.

"But isn't a plan based entirely on assumptions, just a recipe for disaster, after all Garbage in: Garbage out?" While it is true that Business Plans are based on "best guesses," I would take an educated guess over nothing at all, especially a guess made by someone who is allegedly a leader in their field. Most investors do not expect your Business Plan to be correct, especially the financials, but they do anticipate one that is reasonable and well thought out. Further, no VC that I have ever met returns to their portfolio company five years after investment, with the original business plan in hand, in search for things that do not match.

The Bottom Line

You need to write a Business Plan, with emphasis on "YOU". No, it will not be 100 percent accurate. Yes, it will take hundreds of hours. Yes, investors might not read it cover to cover, but without a Business Plan, your ship is sailing not just without a map, but without a compass as well. And although you might accidentally "discover" the new world, it is more likely that you will be lost at sea.

Chapter 18

Love The One You Are With

Originally published February 21, 2007

Being an entrepreneur is tough: up before dawn, emailing at midnight and working non-stop in between. There seems to be no end to the items on your To Do List, which grows exponentially as you garner more success.

So what is an entrepreneur to do in a world where 905 has become 24/7? The answer is simpler than you think – Remember to be good to yourself!

That's right! One of my suggested keys to entrepreneurial success is to be good to yourself. Why, you ask? Because at the heart of your entrepreneurial venture, beside the customers and next to the product is YOU! Hence, you must take care of yourself, or you will be undermining one of the KEY assets of your venture.

> **Wise Words #36**
> *Entrepreneurs should invest in themselves, just as they invest in their staff and their venture.*

Entrepreneurs should invest in themselves, just as they invest in their staff and their business. They should make time once a week, if not daily, to undertake an activity that brings them joy and reminds them why they decided to pursue their path.

In order to help those who might have neglected these types of tasks, I have borrowed and modified a list that my long-time girlfriend, Miss Allie Hughes, created. As an unbelievably brilliant and dedicated clinical social worker assisting young adults with mental illness through the Canadian Mental Health Association, Allie compiled this list to help her clients be good to themselves. I have taken the liberty of adding a few items to her list and modifying some others, but would suggest that you print out this list, tape it to your bulletin board and ensure that you check off a good number of these items daily. After all, much like machinery, if you do not tend to yourself, you will breakdown

Where You Good To Yourself Today? (*The Entrepreneurial Version*)

Have You:

- Had a shower
- Flossed
- Went for a walk
- Got some fresh air
- Asked for a hug
- Made a face in the mirror
- Listened to music
- Smiled in the mirror
- Called a friend
- Saw a friend
- Played with an animal
- Sang out loud
- Hummed
- Got a massage
- Did yoga

- Visualized something good happening
- Got rid of old junk & clutter
- Volunteered
- Ate breakfast
- Bought a new piece of clothing
- Dressed warmly
- Got a pedicure
- Got a manicure
- Took a compliment well
- Watched a good movie
- Let yourself cry
- Ate something sweet
- Finished a project
- Read something
- Solved a problem
- Went to the gym
- Looked up at the stars
- Stopped
- Whistled
- Danced
- Stretched
- Napped
- Cleaned your finger nails
- Washed your hands
- Shaved
- Created something
- Laughed out loud
- Shared a secret
- You-Tubed "newscaster bloopers"
- Got something off your chest
- Apologized

- Confessed
- Fixed something
- Written in your journal
- Sent a hand written thank you note
- Had a bubble bath
- Got enough sleep
- Slept in
- Went on a date
- Kissed someone
- Smelled a flower
- Looked at art
- Went to the park
- Got on a swing
- Got on a teeter-totter
- Put ice in your drink
- Played a sport
- Kicked a stone down the street for fun
- Surfed the net
- Wore something soft and comfy
- Drank enough water
- "Went" when you had to go
- Told someone "I can't"
- Told someone "I'd love to"
- Washed your hair
- Styled your hair
- Brushed your teeth
- Ate some fruit
- Ate some vegetables
- Told a joke
- Skated, skiid, or rollerbladed
- Went swimming

- Did something silly
- Had a cup of tea
- Brushed your hair
- Chatted up a stranger
- Gave to charity
- Recycled
- Learned something new
- Tried to be positive
- Forgave yourself
- Forgave somebody else
- Taught somebody something
- Wrote a poem
- Just lied around
- Played a game
- Looked at photos
- Been honest
- Told a white lie & didn't feel too bad
- Took a deep breath
- Doodled
- Hugged someone
- Said "I love you"
- Had a pillow fight
- Had the courage to say "I don't know"
- Admired your beauty
- Admired nature's beauty
- Fished
- Made a "fart" noise with your mouth
- Made a fart noise with your armpit
- Giggled
- Heard a child giggle
- Hugged yourself

- Practiced something
- Hugged a stuffed animal
- Talked to your doctor
- Put on your cologne or perfume
- Put on deodorant
- Thrown a snowball
- Built a sandcastle
- Had a good debate
- Admired your success
- Went somewhere new
- Noticed something beautiful about the world
- Let something bad just roll off your back
- Listened to the quiet
- Slept with earplugs in
- Put on lip balm
- Put on lotion
- Went without makeup or products
- Used the good soap
- Drank the good wine
- Prayed
- Meditated
- Read philosophy
- Read a trashy magazine
- Read a comic
- Kept a promise
- Blew a bubble
- Participated in any of the following: 3 legged race, potato sack race, egg toss, dunk tank, hot-dog or pie-eating contest, yodeling contest, or human wheelbarrow race
- Screwed up and laughed about it
- Asked for help

- Loved your body
- Not smoked
- Asked for seconds
- Scratched an itch
- Booked a vacation
- Played hooky
- Called in sick
- Put real butter on it
- Put margarine on it instead
- Put on slippers
- Zoned out and daydreamed
- Procrastinated
- Got it done
- Let it go
- Gotten over it
- Decided to change it
- Accepted it the way it is
- Grieved
- Missed somebody
- Let someone "off the hook" even though you had them "dead to rights"
- Stopped when you had enough
- Asked for what you wanted
- Sent it back
- Crank called someone
- Played a practical joke
- Got out in the sun
- Got out of the sun
- Put on sunscreen
- Left an abusive situation
- Left your Blackberry at home, on purpose

- Called home
- Smiled at somebody
- Spent time with your lightlamp
- Did a craft
- Put lots of ketchup on it
- Put chocolate on it
- Got a check-up
- Took your medication/vitamins
- Spent time with your kids
- Got away from your kids
- Made love
- Had sex
- Fooled around
- Kicked it into high gear
- Did something outside your comfort zone
- Went to the shop floor just to hang out with those that make your product
- Tried on expensive shoes
- Did a collage of how you'd like your life to turn out
- Went to a concert
- Called a radio station to request a song
- Floated
- Got a milk moustache
- Made a noise like any of the following: lion / tiger / cheetah / puma / leopard / lynx / cougar / elephant / crow / rooster / dog / horse / pig / dinosaur (preferably T-Rex)
- Screamed to get it out
- Cured your hiccups
- Wore a bright colour
- Asked about your family tree
- Brought "sexy" back

- Tried to either a) beat box, b)break dance, or c) bring it
- Flirted
- Bragged just a tiny bit
- Sent yourself a nice card in the mail – seriously
- Saved some money
- Spent it
- Rapped
- Pretended to be Mohammad Ali
- Let yourself get dirty
- Jumped in a puddle
- Went on a ride
- Got taken on a piggy back / sleigh / horse / motorcycle ride
- Reorganized
- Reprioritized
- Jumped in a lake
- Lied down on the grass
- Had a picnic
- Walked in a creek
- Chanted or repeated a mantra
- Snuggled
- Hired a babysitter
- Said "thank you"
- Told someone "Good Job"
- Talked with an employee who you don't normally speak with
- Sat on a park bench with hot chocolate or cider
- Rode the bus for fun
- People-watched
- Window shopped
- Did a home facial

- Deep conditioned
- Remembered a happy memory
- Lied in the sunbeam
- Put a bow on it
- Got lost on purpose
- Scheduled nothing to do all day
- Opened the door for a stranger
- Laughed at assumptions in your original business plan
- Filled out this list.

The Bottom Line

Although satisfying some of the criteria on this list daily will not guarantee entrepreneurial success, the probability of failing or succeeding at the cost of your happiness increases as this list becomes more neglected. Therefore, this month in honour of Valentine's Day, take the time to show yourself that while there is no "I" in "team," there is definitely a "U" in "entrepreneur".

Wise Words Review

Closing Venture Capital is a lot like consummating a marriage, it takes time for the relationship to mature and blossom. (Pg 1)

The easiest way to get a VC meeting is getting a warm referral from a CEO currently in the VC's portfolio. (Pg 6)

One of the biggest mistakes that entrepreneurs make in pursuing capital is over shopping or shot-gunning their deal. (Pg 9)

An entrepreneur's ability to network can determine whether the venture succeeds or starves to death. (Pg 17)

For any commercial relationship to be sustainable their must be balance. For balance, there must be an alignment of interests. (Pg 19)

By providing utility to someone, you have a better chance of getting fed yourself. (Pg 20)

You should never ask for a favor that is not in their best interest to give, beyond their efficacy, or goes against their goals. (Pg 22)

Double Dipping refers to the ability to generate multiple revenue stems from the same expenditure of resources. (Pg 26)

The ability to pitch in a meaningful, compelling and consist manner is one of the Entrepreneur's most necessary skills. (Pg 37)

Sixty per cent of the investment decision comes down to the quality of Management. (Pg 51)

WISE WORDS

Domain knowledge, vision and passion are critical to a startup, but nothing is ever sold without a sales guy. (Pg 64)

Many investors won't fund a founder they couldn't or wouldn't have a beer with. (Pg 76)

Visual diagrams can serve as a powerful platform for conversation. (Pg 83)

Formulate answers to key investor questions in advance to improve your chances for investment. (Pg 90)

No matter the product, there has to be a need for it. (Pg 91)

You can't be the only one drinking the kool-aid. (Pg 93)

Investors have little appetite for a company that fails to hit milestones. (Pg 95)

Your valuation relies on both intrinsic and extrinsic factors. (Pg 99)

Investors want to verify that the entrepreneur's goals are consistent with theirs. (Pg 102)

Investors tend to risk their money on ventures that are tackling billion dollar sized markets. (Pg 104)

Scalability means revenues accelerate quicker than costs. (Pg 105)

The chances of getting funding go down dramatically if the founders aren't fully committed. (Pg 106)

Strong boards can be an entrepreneur's dream asset or a founders worst nightmare. (Pg 109)

If the Board is too small, you lose the opportunity to maximize their leverage. (Pg 112)

A well rounded management team is made up of equal parts: Business Acumen, Domain Knowledge and Operational Experience. (Pg 113)

When recruiting a Board, seek those with the skills, networks and experiences that management doesn't have. (Pg 119)

If you train yourself to be comfortable in problematic situations you are never caught off guard. (Pg 123)

Before you can focus on victory, you need to set yourself up for it. (Pg 124)

Take the fight to the spot your opponent doesn't want to go. (Pg 126)

You have to be always open to learning new things. You have to be willing to listen to others. (Pg 127)

Creating a business plan is a critical step in any venture. (Pg 135)

A well written business plan gives stakeholders a common place to start a dialogue. (Pg 136)

A business plan assists in identifying the resources you are lacking. (Pg 138)

A good plan concisely conveys managements passion and vision.
(Pg 139)

View your business plan not as a biblical guide but as
a snapshot of strategic belief. (Pg 141)

Entrepreneurs should invest in themselves, just as they invest
in their staff and their venture. (Pg 143)

Index

W

Walden VC, 69
Walking Dead, 33
Walkman, 94
Washington, Kirk, 1, 4, 7
Wikipedia, 84, 124
Wilson, Roger, 70
Wu, Susan, 147

X

Xplane, 87

Y

Yaletown Ventures, 1, 4
YouTube, 131, 135, 138

Z

Znaimer, Sam, 68
Zombie, 33